Field of Light and Shadow

Field of

Light and Shadow

SELECTED AND NEW POEMS
EXPANDED EDITION

DAVID YOUNG

ALFRED A. KNOPF   NEW YORK   2023

THIS IS A BORZOI BOOK
PUBLISHED BY ALFRED A. KNOPF

Some poems in this collection originally appeared in the following works: *Sweating Out the
Winter* (University of Pittsburgh Press, 1969); *Boxcars* (Ecco Press, 1973); *Work Lights: Thirty-
Two Prose Poems* (Cleveland State University Press Poetry Center, 1977); *The Names of a Hare
in English* (University of Pittsburgh Press, 1979); *Foraging* (Wesleyan University Press, 1986);
Earthshine (Wesleyan University Press, 1988); *The Planet on the Desk* (Wesleyan University
Press, 1991); *Night Thoughts and Henry Vaughan* (Ohio State University Press, 1994); *At the
White Window* (Ohio State University Press, 2000); and *Black Lab* (Alfred A. Knopf, 2006).

Some of the poems in the "New Poems" section previously appeared in the following:
"The Dead from Iraq," "Reading Yannis Ritsos in November," and "The Void," from
"Occasional Sonnets" in *ABZ;* "Mother's Day" in *The Journal of General Internal Medicine;*
"Why I Translate" in *Poetrysky;* "Graveyard" in *Red Wheelbarrow;* and "One Hundred Billion
Neurons in My Brain" in *Visions International*. "The Dead from Iraq" also appeared in
The Best American Poems of 2008, edited by Charles Wright and David Lehman and
"Graveyard" was published as a broadside from North River Press in 2009.

Some of the poems in the "New Poems II (2022)" section previously appeared in the following:
"Reading Old Letters on a Rainy Morning" in *Miramar;* "Her Voice Has Vanished," "Since
Galileo Started Something," and "Edge, Rim, Frontier, Limit," in *Red Wheelbarrow*.

Library of Congress Cataloging-in-Publication Data
Young, David, [date]
Field of light and shadow : selected and new poems / by David Young. — 1st ed. p. cm.
ISBN 978-1-5247-1233-4
I. Title.
ps3575.o78f54 2010
811'.54—dc22
2010001797

Cover photograph by C. Jones/Latentseen
Cover design by Carol Devine Carson

Manufactured in Canada
Published September 7, 2010
First Paperback Edition, January 31, 2023

Contents

from Work Lights: Thirty-Two Prose Poems

from The Names of a Hare in English

from The Planet on the Desk

from Night Thoughts and Henry Vaughan

from At the White Window

from Black Lab

New Poems (2010)

New Poems II (2022)

from

Sweating Out the Winter

Late Summer: Lake Erie

Nearly a year since word of death
broke off the summer: as if a goddess
you followed respectfully
should turn and stun you with her look.

We can go back to Old Woman Creek,
easy canoeing except where lotus
and water lily choke the way:
rose mallows massed on the banks, around
bends the sudden rise of ducks,
invisible bitterns, the silent, ponderous
heron, our kingfisher escort,
and, under the still, flowering
surface, death: the orange carp
crowd toward the killer lake.

I swore I'd write no letters to the dead.
It's only myself I want to tell
things are about the same. The wind
still pounds and stumbles around the cottage,
the lake is streaked and rumpled, dead
fish wash up to the beach, our summer
is the same sweet, easily murdered pleasure.
I wade in the supple breakers, I'll
paddle again on the creek. Now,
this morning, I walk to the road;
all to the south the dazed, hot landscape lies,
under its piled thunderheads,
dreaming of love and survival.

1964

The Man Who Swallowed a Bird

Happened when he was yawning.
A black or scarlet bird went down his throat
and disappeared, and at the time
he only looked foolish, belched a feather;
the change took time.

But when we saw him again in the
half-dusk of a summer evening
he was a different man. His eyes
glittered and his brown hands
lived in the air like swallows;
knowledge of season lit his face
but he seemed restless. What he said
almost made sense, but from a distance:

> *Once I swallowed a bird,*
> *felt like a cage at first, but now*
> *sometimes my flesh flutters and I think*
> *I could go mad for joy.*

In the fall he vanished. South,
some said, others said dead. Jokes
about metamorphosis were made. Nonetheless,
some of us hear odd songs.
    Suppose
you press your ear against the morning air,
above and on your left you might
hear music that implies without a word
a world where a man can absorb a bird.

More About Skills

I saw myself talking
at a distance, hands busy

with the air: scooping it,
shaping it, drawing it out,

and brushing it away,
a story of hands and arms.

The words were lost like smoke
but the gestures were ancient

signs that I took to say:
how do we know our medium

except we divide it
with our hands, breaking its bread,

pouring its thin wine. Here
is a batch I have gathered,

before it disperses, inspect
it, sift and caress it,

carry it weightless on your
wrists, your unmapped palms,

drink it, spring in the blood,
return it in smoky words,

words that beget gestures,
gestures assembling the air.

Segal

The girl who sits on the bed
facing the window while her lover sleeps

leans, hands on the mattress, into
a blue, enormously late, light,

her arms, face, breasts all turning
blue while she thinks about nothing

but simply carries her sorrow
and is unconscious of her beauty

while in the room where the sculptor
has put her, the light comes slowly

back to bright, as her white skin
grows whiter, her flesh more solid,

she, her lover, the bed, unstained
by color or darkness, polar, thick,

as if the light could take us unaware
when we knew least that we were what

we hoped we'd be, calm and intact;
as if the light could give us what we lacked.

Poem About Hopping

Rabbits in Alabama hop
into clumps of Syrian grass
to nibble the stalks, thinking of
sorghum, hardly noticing autumn.

Along the Great Divide the bighorn
sheep hop casually from rock to
rock in the wind and glare, seriously
considering leaping silver rivers, as

salmon in crazy waters jump
upstream for love—oh it's
a nervous country. When you
walk through stubble, the hub

of a wheel with grasshopper
spokes, or sit over bowls of excited
cereal, what can you say to your heart
but, Down sir, down sir, down?

Two Renewal Poems

1. THE LINE

What weather is this?
My body is heavy, real; it walks
out of the house, into the wind.
My small son watches from the window;
I wave and walk away.
A blue jay stalls
above a spruce. My
forehead touches the cold glass.
My father waves
and walks away.

2. THE CIRCLE

Driving across Iowa
in the corn-green light, you
sometimes come across
between the road and pasture
a knee-high gush of water
from a deep artesian well
rising and tumbling into itself
in the raw sun, cold and sweet.

You stand at the center of summer,
your life rising and falling.

Take a tin cup from the fencepost.
Drink.

Nineteen Sixty-Three

The year the president was killed
Was the same my friend was shot
On a Washington street one night
For his white skin and wallet.

What we can't bear we bury.
I got so I thought I could
Stand the abruptness if only
There were some final word.

But when he returned in a dream,
Dying and white like Gracchus,
And there was a chance to explain,
We were both shy and speechless.

Then I grew light with wonder
Watching beside the bed.
My stubbornness fell away
For I thought I understood

That he wouldn't elect to live
Here at the end of the myth
If he could, and I smiled and said,
"You're the President of Death."

In Memoriam: Newell Ellison

from

Boxcars

The Boxcar Poem

The boxcars drift by
clanking

they have their own
speech on scored
wood sheet
metal their own
calligraphy
Soo Line
they say in meadows
Lackawanna quick at crossings
Northern Pacific, a
nightmurmur, Northern
Pacific

even empty
they carry
in dark corners
among smells of wood and sacking
the brown wrappings of sorrow
the rank straw of revolution
the persistence of war

and often
as they roll past
like weathered obedient
angels you can see
right through them
to yourself
in a bright
field, a crow
on either shoulder.

Three for the Moon

1.

A bluegreen January dusk
and the full moon
risen
        beyond the water tower

Leaving the office
suddenly foolish with joy
I have one thought:
we don't
deserve
this earth.

2.

Tonight the moon is not an onion
above a yellow Spanish town

or a fresh cabbage
over a Russian village

tonight the moon has one name
and no figure but its own

though my arm is more than an arm
my briefcase a sleepy farm.

3.
Say it is dawn in the mountains
after the shortest night of summer
and I kneel at a pool
still in the shadows
watching the last four stars
rock slightly
                    not winking out
but starting to join
the larger light

That is the feeling of the moon
as I drive home, flooding,
tumbling, part of the light
bright on the ice of the creek
round and fragrant in the pines
this water tower
looking glass
floodlight
moon!

Homing

1.

"Attacks are being launched
to clean out enemy sanctuaries . . ."

Watching the president's features
I'm childlike,
homesick.

For what?
A warm basement in Des Moines
a den in a thicket
the dense invisible pulsar
in the huge Crab Nebula . . .

2.

The visiting poet
has been on the bottle
all over Ohio. Come back
to the state he was born in,
missing his wife and New York apartment,
he rolls his big flushed
baby's head and whispers
"I want my mother."

Unwilling to be left alone
unwilling to talk to us
he recites for a while like a bright child
and goes to bed hugging his misery.
Next morning he grabs a bus south.
I wave goodbye in the exhaust.
Everything's shaking.

3.

The jackrabbit flushed by the car
is scared. In stiff
zigzag bounds he cuts
along the highway, then swerves suddenly
across an open field. Eighty yards to trees.
An easy shot.
But he knows
where he's going.

4.

Pedaling home I glimpse
a sea-green boxcar
drifting along the tracks
by itself
and my Uncle Bert, the best
farmer in the family,
dressed in fresh overalls
clinging to the ladder—
is he waving me off
or beckoning?

At dusk
a half-dozen crows come
slowly over
the factory, the dairy
heading back
to their roost in the swamp
too far in
for hunters to follow.

In the yard
the smoke bush sings:
You have
nowhere to turn to
now.

5.

Heavy and calm
summer rolls in
grass rises around us
like mother love
clouds build
in great treeshapes
yellow, peach, violet,
disperse or crash in storms
and the trees, cloudlike,
boil up in the wind
jittery, blazing green.

A black-and-yellow bird
—whose name escapes me—
startles me into pleasure
as I walk near the quarry
thinking of war, of the steady
state theory, of my children and
my parents, standing together
at Stonehenge
that Easter Sunday
my wife's mother
died of cancer.

Goldfinch! He flies up. Wings
beating, is he in
my family, are we
home?

6.

Sometimes I have to remember
to notice my children. Today

my daughter brought me a tulip
waxy and white, its petals
about to scatter—
hugging her I caught
in the fragrance of her hair
a smell of kinship.

Later we all
drove to the country
to see the green
sprouts in the long
ploughed fields
the lambs, chickens, earthworms
who live so surely
on and in their earth, and when
we were tired
I glanced at the stacking clouds
and said
"Let's go home."

And we went
together, down the paved road,
and not
as each of us would go
some time, alone,
rushing
across the black fields
toward the moon
that old bone
floating
out beyond evening.

May 1970
Cambodia, Kent State, Jackson State

In Heaven

There
where the self is a fine powder
drifting free

simply by wishing
you can be
whatever you like:
a fish swiped by a bear's paw
a woman whose son is insane
a spear in the side of a tiger

They do not feast there
they do not hymn perfection or
the ecstasies of love

for their own reasons
they care most
to assume the shapes of suffering:

helicopters swooning into clearings
through crossfire, burning

or an old hare
limping across
a stripped field
in late November.

Mandelstam

"He had difficulty breathing . . .
Osip breathed heavily; he was catching air with his lips."
—ANNA AKHMATOVA

1. AT THE CAMP

Hell freezing over. To keep sane
he studies the tiniest sensations
such as the touch of a necklace
of dry dead bees around a woman's neck.
Having said that, he can mention
honey, then speak of sunlight.
He studies his hands. Stalin's a swine.
Nadezhda's head is a beehive, full of poems.
He licks his lips to whisper one.
They're chapped. His breath is smoke.
His ears stick out as if to catch
even the noise of a candle flame.
Frostbite will get them first.
A sledge goes past, stacked high.
Better not look. Ice lies in piles,
shoals, hummocks. Memories of Warsaw,
Paris, Petersburg, the warm Crimea
keep their distance, northern lights,
or the swords of half-drunk Cossacks
whirling through stupid dances.
He lives on garbage, is never warm, will die.

2. THE TEAR, 1938

A tear is floating over Moscow
swollen, seeking a home, a mirror.

Tear, take my advice, get lost.
Those onion domes don't want you,

the rivers are solid glass
the earth's a cake of permafrost

even those women wrapped in shawls
would gulp you like a drop of vodka.

Better go east, better follow
that long railway to Asia;

you can survive, little crystal,
in the glossy eye of a reindeer

on the bear's nose as he sleeps
dreaming sun into honey

in the fur of the wolf who runs
through the endless, falling snow.

3. NADEZHDA WRITES A LETTER

Nonchalant, the sun goes off
and then returns. You won't.
Except in dreams, old films
flickering, buzzing when
your lips whisper, catching air,

making poems, sound tracks, and
I reach to touch you in the dark.

You left in a hurry, shrugging,
framed by policemen.
And your journey? The camps,
the cattle cars, beatings, stinks—
I see your forehead wrinkle, tongue thicken,
I turn away. Tears sting.
Maybe we should have jumped
hand in hand through the window!

It's warm in the Kremlin, there's music.
Stalin's small eyes glitter
his mustache is greasy with shashlik
he drinks, smashing his glass:
if the universe
makes any sense
how did we get from those fine-drawn
Petersburg afternoons
through the bonfires and rifle shots
of that marvelous revolution
to *this*?

But listen, Osip,
the joke's on them. Poems survive.
Your costly whispers carry.
They coexist with the state
like sunlight.
                          I can
still hear you, Osip:
catching air, your high-strung voice
speaks for the frozen and forgotten
saying, it *was* their earth, it was
their earth. Purges don't change that.

Though that's dim comfort tonight
as I sit with my bread and soup
and the wind off the wrinkled plains
howls like a man without a tongue.
Brave man, who shredded the death warrants
of a leather-jacketed terrorist
and then ran wild through the Russian cold,
my warm sun, shrunk to star,
it's a stiff, black world
you left behind.

Thoughts of Chairman Mao

1.

Holding black whips
the rulers rode
in the blue hills.

But the peasants were everywhere and nowhere,
a soft avalanche, gathering
courage; in famines
we ate the mules, tasting vinegar,
lived among rocks above the passes,
and gradually became an army
red flags snapping in the wind
and I wrote of "a forest of rifles,"
and of heroes strolling home
against a smoky
sunset.

2.

Wars merge like seasons;
sometimes over hot wine
the old campaigners try to remember
who we were fighting that winter
on this plateau, that plain,
and whether we won.

It blurs . . .
miles in boxcars
doors wedged open
miles across blue-shadowed snow.
Hungry evening.

Artillery at the river
bodies in the rice fields
a black truck on its side
burning . . .

At night we could hear the gibbons
calling each other up the valley.
When there was a rest or a vista
someone would write a poem.
It blends and blurs:
conferences melonseeds sabotage
dungfires treaties mosquitoes
my great red army on the march
blinking in the sunshine.

3.
Now it is changed.
I am the giant in the pageant,
toothy, androgynous, quilted.

To the slow roll of drums
my effigy speaks to the people
of harvests, steel mills, stars.

In the puppet shows I battle
enemies of the state
sometimes with blows and curses
sometimes with love and flowers
while Marx pops up to hug me
and Lenin takes my arm.

I would have done it
with poems! Instead
I have come to be
a red book, a pumped-up myth,

from Long March to Big Swim
surfacing, always surfacing:
said to have gone
miles through golden water
wrestled the Yangtze and won,
water god, flower king, rice prince;

the current takes me on
and it is no small thing
riding these tides, wave upon
wave of love, smiling, unspeaking,
ten thousand miles of mountains and water,
a chanting race, a skin on history,

until the people rise and go,
dispersing me.

4.
At the end I enter a small room.
Stalin is standing there alone
hands behind his back
gazing out the window.

We link arms. We merge.

And the rulers ride the blue hills
holding their black whips high.

Ohio

Looking across a field
at a stand of trees
—more than a windbreak
less than a forest—
is pretty much all
the view we have

in summer it's lush
in winter it gets
down to two or
three tones   for
variety
there might be
an unpainted barn
water patches
a transmission tower

yet there's a lot
to see
        you could sit
all day on the rusty
seat of a harrow
with that view before you
and all the sorrows
this earth has seen
sees now   will see
could pass through
you like a long
mad bolt of lightning
leaving you drained
and shaken
still
at dusk

the field would be
the same and the growing
shadows of the trees
would cross it toward you
until you rose   your heart
pounding with joy and walked
gladly through the weeds
and toward the trees.

Love Song

for Chloe

I guess your beauty doesn't
bother you, you wear it easy
and walk across the driveway
so casual and right it makes
my heart weigh twenty pounds
as I back out and wave
thinking She's my summer
peaches, corn, long moondawn dusks
watermelons chilling in a tub
of ice and water: mirrored there
the great midsummer sky
rolling with clouds and treetops
and down by the lake
the wild canaries
swinging on the horsemint
all morning long.

Chromos

1.
Why have I pinned this postcard up?

Orange flames lick
the volcano's purple rim
under a plum-blue sky.

Wow.
I picture your face and breasts
lit by that glow. I decide
we will visit Hawaii.

2.
Like a strange church the jet
sits in silhouette
under a dark grape dawn.

The runway looks deserted;
maybe the pilot, yawning,
is climbing into his harness.

At the horizon a wild
incandescence, yellow-white

as if the world was starting to burn.

3.
In a slate-green night the lighthouse
pokes its beam at a right
angle to itself.

The beam looks solid
a dowel, a tube
a flattering self-portrait
of the lighthouse.

4.
The sky is navy-blue
the Flatiron Building's a handsome
reddish-brown, speckled
with tiny yellow squares.

A lemon on a divan, the moon
watches from puffy clouds
thinking trout? basket? lightship?

5.
What I want to do
is fan out a handful
of new cards, dazzlers.
Take a card:

Geysers of light
that mate around cities

Mountains waxed and polished

A picture of the well
in the bottom of the sky

The gears of light toward which
we fall so gently as they knit

The blades, teardrops, sphincters
of lampshine

It's our appetite for light, it's how
the world keeps pushing back
the world we must invent,
all that give and take . . .
Take a card:

  Those places I hoped to live:
  the Residence of Dorothy Lamour,
  Ethel Farley's Inn, the Willow
  Banks Hotel, and most of all
  the Golden Temple of Jehol,
  are ablaze, blooming, collapsing . . .

By their light I can just
make out this postcard
this chromolithograph
this poem.

A Calendar: The Beautiful Names of the Months

January
On this yearly journey two
faces are better—a weary
woman, a wary man.

February
Where the earth goes
to run a fever. The care's good.
Herbs brew. The rooms are airy.

March
Bridge curving over a swamp.
A bruise that smarts, the long
patience of an army.

April
Neither grape nor apple.
Any monkey, a pearly sprig,
a prism. Flute notes.

May
The arch opens. Crowds.
Goats, babies, vowels, and
the wind, permitting anything.

June
A jury rises.
The moons of Jupiter
set. Bugs, berries, prairie grass.

July
Jewelers snooze on the grass,
one eye open for the tall
constellation-poppies.

August
Clearing your throat of dust.
Wading in lagoons . . . algae,
hot bursts of wind.

September
Lives away from his brothers,
gentle-tempered, a little solemn.
Bears pests, eats peas and beets.

October
Cold roots and a fresh-caught owl
rocked on a cot.
An orange boot.

November
Toothache and memory.
Nine women. Overdressed beavers.
No new members.

December
Something decent, easy.
Frozen meekness. Wax. A good
end, an ember, then ten of them.

Teddy Roosevelt

Stumping again it hurts by god
have traveled all around the tattooed
lady my country looking for the right
spot to raise the banner of straw some
water tower some windmill though my big head
aches and I miss the wax works greatly
clouds hang above old toads strange poppies
acetylene evenings seven fireflies solitude
blue pastures where a bull paws up cool soil
dragging my bad leg through the spirit village
seized by the women covered with sycamore leaves
as if I was the corn dog the potato man
no one knows me understands my language
the pulse of the tattooed lady is bad
I fear for her life I fear for her death
I would give her both if I could but I sit
here on the porch of this rainsmoke penthouse
while the music rises like mosquito smudge
through which a red sun comes rolling rolling

Woodrow Wilson

I pull on the tight clothes and go walking
rectitude misting around my figure
carrying the book of shadows a low moon
crosses the powerstations the refineries
and in the needle mountains there are lakes
so cold and clear that the dead who sit
on the bottom in buggies and machine-gun nests
look up past the trout that nibble their shoulders
to see the eclipse begin the dime-sized shadow
sliding across the sun the insects settling
around the bears in their yokes the antelopes
acting out all their desires old lady
who smothers her young in her iron robes
you have wrung my thin neck a thousand times
and taken my pinchnose glasses but
I come back again with the gliding Indians
settlers who have forgiven all their tools
the shabby buffaloes wild sheep wapiti
the inland sea that looks at the sky all day
with only a widgeon's wake to disturb it
the V dividing away from itself
all night under trembling constellations

from Water Diary

walking the tracks in early March
thinking where would I store a handcar
we ponder the fast clouds my son and I
and stare at winter's house   look down:
smashed grass gravel in a pool rainrings
wet rust on the tracks the creek rushing
no trains today no setting out arriving
the wind bucketing off through the trees
and sunset a skin of ice on each red puddle

≈≈

my eyes   heavy the plumtree burning
muscles in my neck twist and I
reach toward you   even in summer air
your face is cool   a winter window
steelwork   we drive off the city lies
in haze behind but this
hot mist is everywhere
unsketching the little towns
and the fields with their cows and flies

≈≈

the punt bumps the bank
jump ashore kick the boat back
to circle in the current
the black cinders crunch
here's the cottage the old man
sleeps at his desk everything's
familiar the blue door the sweater
over a chair the picture of a glacier
the ginger beer the luger on the rug

the wind breathing in the fireplace
wells cisterns rainwater
lady lady lady lady

≈≈

o stiff cadets your buttons shine
the rows of corn the aimed November wind
ran over a black snake near the quarry
going the wrong direction the daylight
racing across the clouds the dusty city
where a whole brass band got lost on purpose
or the sky where long blue moving vans
park to study aviation and the stars
what do you know about river currents
wheat sperm fountain lions drill towers
what it means to be human stop it at once

≈≈

these lemons are packed in ice
and shipped to skating rinks in the Dakotas
or imagine a river of very chilly whiskey
lumber barons along the banks
we have all seen helicopters flying sideways
data processing centers in Tennessee
astrakhan collars rain pocking snow
every direction is good and today
it has something to do with the cedar waxwing
seen at the feeder while I read Shakespeare
like starting over in the arms of water
"your body finds naturally its liberty"

≈≈

the Empress seized the throne by unsavory means
and the poets strolled morose in the cashew orchards
young men were ridiculed by the thistle gate
while purple swallows flew in the snowy foothills
it is all the same   time   all the same
"Who now remembers," mused the Secretary of Rituals
"the monkey chariots that drew the courtesans
among the jade fountains and the pruned bamboo?"
and as he spoke, gazing out at his pepper plants
the invention of movable type occurred
and the waters of immortality faded from view

≈≈≈

the olive-colored water spoke again
'49 Packards drew up to the Turkey Shoot
The Autobiography of Honolulu   listen
the water spoke volumes and the fruit
carved by the light of mutton tallow
made a perfectly good prize for the best
drop of water sliding down the cheek
imagine all this as a sort of waterclock
though not the kind that drips or burns
rising the months rising the mist rising
the spirits rising the mountains rising
meadowlarks constellations words

≈≈≈

water is beads on the eaves steam
from a manhole cover most of my body
tears saliva urine sweat meadows flooding
what the spinning windmill pumps what
rains and bounces on mountain slopes
sinks into darkening earth is lost
and found again in giant summer clouds

shapechanger fog where glacier meets ocean
yesterday dew all over the freightcar
rimefrost today swamp pools tomorrow
imagination colorless and holding every color
window and mirror holding any image
the green creek wrinkling with a mallard
settling toward its own reflection in the sky
is time as line as circle is the snowman sinking
back inside himself is what can't be named is water

≈≈

wrinkle wrinkle movie star the ice bird sang
she put her marvelous foot on the next step down
and shock waves traveled the length of her body
at the banquet there was a swan carved out of ice
and several people dreamed of riding it naked
into that distance where light is no longer king
and nothing moves in the endless black lagoons
but darkness itself with a faint and dangerous slopping

≈≈

for several days the temperature stood so low
that at last we could walk on water   and we did
the creek creaked softly talking to itself
along the banks through harmless fissures
we brushed some snow aside and peered down through
but could see nothing not water not even ourselves
there was a strange sensation of wrinkles and darkness
we knocked on the stuff   for entrance   for luck
and an old man spoke from a book
"why can't mind and matter
be more like wind and water?"
we looked up   snow was wobbling toward us
through miles and miles and miles of soundless air

from

Work Lights

Thirty-Two Prose Poems

The Poem Against the Horizon

In a dim room above the freightyards, next to an old brass bed, an angel is taking off his wings. He winces a little as he eases the straps that run down into his chest: the beat of the wings is the beat of the heart.

Out of harness, the heart rolls over now. Panting like a wrestler. Such love, such soaring! Spokane and back. So good to come down, home to this room with the stained lace curtains and the sound of switch engines. So good to remove the wings, the love, the yoke the blood must wear as it paces, oxlike, the circle of its day . . .

He sleeps on his side in the overalls he was too tired to take off. Outside the window, rain runs and drips from the eaves. Overhead, the wind and the black sky belong to someone else.

Four About the Letter P

Ponies grazing where there's wild garlic. "Only those who have smelled the breath of cows pasturing . . ." Thirty-four electric shock treatments. Fifty comas. Dances of women while men are away fighting. Whistling. Bumblebees around the salt. Scolding. While snow billows and blows through the orchards and windbreaks of the family farm, he moves quietly through the house, smearing blood on the walls and doorposts.

•

Let's say a white peony. In a jar. Water. Evening and the moon rising like a great engraving. No, like the face of a sleeper. That's better. The housewife peeking out through her curtain while I ring her doorbell. We have to feed ourselves. Ants. Snails. We have to move around, even if the feeling we get is of wandering through a cold cathedral where we know we will encounter the face of the sleeper we are not allowed to photograph or describe. "Julie and her mother were at this time desperate people." Hear the bells. Open your eyes. It's the face, it's just the peony. Petals dropping on the polished rosewood.

•

Hauling a cake of ice from the icehouse, hosing off the sawdust, shaving it to slush that is packed around the can and dasher and sprinkled with rock salt, taking turns with the crank, doing this every Sunday morning through a whole summer so that some hundred people may have ice cream with chokecherry sauce, and never once thinking "This is a piece of the river."

•

How are the potatoes doing? From the field where you have come to inspect them, you can see the lights of the farmhouse not far off. Getting old, you think. Getting cold. Swear on this stone you will not steal yams. Thunder brings them to the surface. Long pigs run loose through the woods. We sit on a veranda, sipping punch. "Magic," the psychiatrist says, "is contagious." Someone snorts. Soft moss, and the sound of a river. And pigeons, rose-gray like the winter woods, rising up startled.

Four About Heavy Machinery

A huge cement truck turns the corner, and you get the full impact of its sensuality. Those ruts on the road and in the lawn! Even at night the cement plant has a strange energy, drawing adolescents to stare through its fences, causing the night watchman to shine his light nervously among the parked and sleeping mixers. Still, from those fluid beginnings and slow revolutions, the cement itself forms the pale and stony squares of sidewalk. Reassuring. Roller skates, hopscotch, salted ice. Then the slow cracking from the tree roots below and we are back to sensuality again.

•

Cranes are not to be compared with trees, not with their almost Scandinavian sense of the importance of duty and power. Sometimes the face is very far from the heart, and the one thing you would like to do—lie down next to that beautiful passing stranger, for instance—is the thing that seems least possible. So you sway against the gray sky, pretending to a stiffness you do not feel. The building you helped create rises toward you, filled with the sounds of hammering and the strange shine of work lights.

•

To take some tutoring from pumps, I said. I was thinking about the windmill, that swaying, clanking lecturer. Slow cows come to drink from the tank. We filled it, didn't we, harvesting water from weather, not by bringing it down from the sky like rain but up from the earth like oil. Now roll up your blue sleeve and plunge your arm into that tank. If you clench and unclench your fist regularly you can learn something about the submersible pump, beating down there where weather is a dream.

•

We have strong feelings about bulldozers, their buzzing and scraping, their clumsy abruptness, their way of tipping saplings into piles of burnable roots and brush. Our faces get vinegary when we think of it. But the bull-dozer's point of view is remarkably different. The bulldozer thinks of itself as a lover. It considers that its loved one, from whom it is separated, is wrapped in many short, soft buttery strips of leather. It imagines itself removing these worn leather wrappings, one at a time and with great tenderness, to get at the body of the loved one. Perverse, you will say. But see, you have already entered the life of the bulldozer; your hands reach for the next piece of leather. Shrubs and young trees go under.

Four About Metaphysics

Who can hold a fire in his hand? You spread your fingers. Ideally, they should be made of a substance like cork, and your palm a substance like hooves. Or antlers. A stag can poke his horns right into a furnace, can't he? Even if he can't, he probably thinks he can, whereas we feel vulnerable in the presence of vast spaces, extreme conditions. That far-flung glitter through which the midget spaceship floats. Or the frosty Caucasus. Or the snapped axle of a covered wagon halfway across the desert. Or the excitement of seeing whales surface by lantern light. All around you. In the dark Pacific. If you didn't have to consider the boat capsizing and the light going out. If you were the boat and your hand its own unquenchable lantern.

•

A glass of water and an onion for his supper, the Spanish visionary sat at his table in the future. Ultimate secrets were streaming from the monastery. A rowboat was crossing the very blurred lake. Sex, for him, was just an impolite kind of staring. But the blue-eyed countess did not seem to mind. Millions of things sought to claim his attention, and he tried to look beyond them. Remembering this sentence: "The sea is as deepe in a calme as in a storm."

•

To one side a thin church, flying a flag or a pair of pants. In the distance a castle from which a flock of rooks streams up in a spreading wedge. Someone fumbling with a barrel. And at a long table before a peeling house, people are talking, eating, fighting, kissing. Noticed by a dog, one man is vomiting. A group of musicians can be seen through the smoke from the cooking fire. About to appear from over the hill, someone like Tamburlaine or Genghis Khan.

•

"How fortunate for Alabama," I thought. I was turning the pages of a book that resembled a piece of ice. Rapidly, as if I feared it would melt. I passed the song, the recipe, the sermon, the code, and the questionnaire. I passed the sketch of the wrestler, flexing his muscles and sobbing. I passed the poem about shooting stars and Puritan names. I was searching for the story that begins: "God was not even allowed to touch Mary. It seemed to him sometimes that if he could just take her face in his hands, the world would reassemble itself with excitement. But he did not. Meanwhile, the seed . . ." And so on. I could not find that story. I came instead to this.

Four About Mummies

Just one pause, in the sane and sleepy museum, is enough. You see the box, with its lid askew, the bone among ancient rags, it dawns on you that the face is not a mask. Now you will be related to it all your life. It will meet you by starlight in the courtyards of sleeping cities. Dressing or undressing your body, you will remember that box, face, rags. And in the horror movies, as you watch its caricature strangle and abduct the foolish archeologists, your smile will tighten and then vanish.

•

In the doctor's office there is a chart of the circulatory system. A blue-and-red thicket grows, but the figure it inhabits is otherwise white and blank; and the hands are spread, as if imploring. But communication is next to impossible. It is said they have their own language, a compound of muffled odors in which they converse like birds. If you were patient and had a keen enough nose, a dark pyramid would be filled with a melancholy, spicy twittering.

•

Egypt's national pastime, given their history, skill, and climate. But we must not forget other nations. Some will have heard of certain North and South American native practices. A few may at least have an inkling of the Irish mummies, safe in their cradles of peat. But what of the Russian mummies, famous in their lifetimes as hypochondriacs? Or the Tartar mummies, poised against horizons on their petrified steeds? Nomads who follow migrations must leave even their dying behind, but the rare accidental mummies of the Lapps somehow contrive to keep up with the reindeer, and are sometimes even seen leading the vast, milling herds across the spring-washed tundra.

•

The body of the loved one, yes, tears and tar, to soak it, to wrap it, removing each organ except the heart, to fill the cavity with spices, to wrap each organ carefully and return it, to swaddle, to bandage, to blur. Does any happiness exceed this? Recall the simple pleasure of draping a shawl around someone's shoulders. And then the box: the façade, the mirror that dignifies, gaily painted, a boat, a boot, a gorgeous wooden nightgown. All of it then to be stowed in the dark where even the explorer's torch cannot reach. There, in perfect silence, with the wrapped cat, the mummied hawk, the dishes of preserved food. Don't dismiss it: *only a fool or a god would shut the book of the dead.*

Kohoutek

In a broad field on a clear night you might stare at the sky quite uselessly, and with expanding dismay. I had the luck to encounter the comet on a gray morning when I was doing next to nothing in an upstairs room. I may have been restless and shaky, but my attention was steady as a trout. Outside, the plane trees began to stir. Then the mirror gave a small tremor. The comet was in the closet! Shaggy and silent. I glanced outside. The same pigeons were walking on the brown corrugated roof next to a skylight. But for a few moments, all the terrifying diffuseness—of matter, of winter light, of interest and love, of the Great Plains and the galaxies themselves—was just exactly bearable!

from

The Names of a Hare in English

Two Views of the Cathedral

1. DAY

Shoulderstones, blockstacks, peaks:
we put it up to catch our breath.
Thumbs, antlers, ferns and flying bones:
we put it up to catch the light.
A million thorns to house a rose,
another mask for God. And then a mind
hushed for the few thin sounds of dream:
the knicker-knack of pigeons in the frieze,
the lunk of something closing in the crypt,
while a woman folds a large white cloth
in the wet yard behind the apse.

2. NIGHT

Uneven candle crescent round the Virgin.
Casket time. The verger sees his breath.
High in the nave, the hunchback sees it all:
history is a slow march down the aisle, is
the countess sobbing in her heavy cloak.
Here a knight sat and felt his throat
fill up with blood. A crunch under my boot:
frost? mortar? salt? I tip my forehead back:
no roof, just dusty stars above . . .
We build. On the numb stone called fear
We fit the heavy one called love.

Nineteen Forty-Four

Dragging a rake, my Uncle Donald
surveys his Victory Garden:

peaceful and green,
all Minneapolis is at war . . .

Since I am seven, that's mostly
cereal box Messerschmitts,
Tojo cartoons, the bombers I draw
sailing through popcorn flak,
bad dreams, brownouts,

and the small cigarette machine
my father and Donald roll smokes with
as they sit up to grumble
at Roosevelt, winning again . . .

Countries of silence. Hand on my heart
I moon to return, searching for signs,
gnats in November, submarines
at rest on the harbor floor.

Then all at once I have done it!
I stand on the corner of Queen Street.
Five o'clock. The nations of the dead.
Mr. Kipke is whistling for his cat
and a light shines across the street
in the bedroom of the boy
with the bullet-shattered spine.

I sidle, thrilled, down our alley,
floating, loose as a ghost.
At our picket gate I find

my father, his back to me.
Is he pondering the war
or my brother, soon to be born?
I could touch his shoulder and ask him
but both of us are fading
as the city shines, all mystery,
and the garden sits empty in twilight:
pine needles, vines, brown leaves,
simple American shadows.

"Other Forms Were Near": Five Words

HONEYGUT (a word for tripe)
Below the graded green of tree, bush, weeds,
it's silent—barn-cathedrals of quiet, but
no space: rooms all wall, jam-packed with roots (white sprays,
hard tentacles), pebbles, sandgrains, humus,
tiger-striped tons of rock, pods of water and gas . . .

When you wake in the morning, rumpled and stunned,
the crumbs around your eyes are there to tell you
where you were lying all night, what you were practicing.

OAT
Yeats stands near his old-hat tower in the twilight;
everything talks to itself—the river over its rocks, the moorhens,
cricket and cowbell, wind in the chimney flue. What he's gaping at:
the Great Pyramid, trembling like a bubble above the trees.

"Willie is booming and buzzing like a bumblebee,"
said Maud Gonne to a friend. "That means he is writing something."
Who can he talk to when he's neither here nor there? Mumbling,
gaping. As the specters billow and fade. Ripe mummy wheat.

BABOON
Today a summer thundershower makes her think
of packs of sacred apes. Long hair, a kind of skidding run.
Isn't the animal mirror best? Those hours in the zoo
watching the young gorilla's hands: black leather work gloves.

The trees drip very strangely.
A robin runs across the lawn.

Bright eye. Serpent mound.
The breathing next to your ear.

HAZE

Old, you were dozing at a window and woke up.
A stranger stood in the yard, the moon behind him,
so that you couldn't see his face. Then you recalled
watching a kingfisher from a canal boat: it was as if
that blue pulse tore straight through you. We're best

when the world shines us through like that. At night
knee-deep in mist, the traveler pauses at a cottage,
straining to catch his face in the empty casement.

INSECT

Cow skull, washtub. Sunday-supplement portrait. Gloomy greatness.
The poem's place in the world was "never in dispute,"
they said. Any more than a blizzard. Or a candle.

When the dead walk, do they need to use their feet?
How gradual it seems, going to sleep each night,
instar after instar. I pace my study, looking for a book.
The snowstorm settles in its globe. The small bright flame
is nearly independent of its wick.

How Music Began

Well the wind blew so hard
that the sea blistered and snapped.
Even the boulders were squeaking.

Trolls scuffled and spat, whacking thick
bones on hollow oaks, screaming for meat,
and birds nattered in every thicket.

Women in birth pangs howled. Bitter couples
shattered cups, jugs, and beakers, while children
slithered on ice among grit and cinders.

●

Then thunder set off the landslide.
Bushes with dead birds tumbled
through blasted air. You couldn't hear

how bones and trees were splintered,
how boulders struck sparks, how the ice
burst, taking some of the children.

●

Then quiet grew up. Like cave pools,
cocoons. Like very old temples at noon.
Nursing. Fruitfall. Sketching the buffalo.

And then it was easy to consider
smoke a bird twisting up
that might sing as the earth got smaller.

Three Time-Trips

1.

My shoes crush acorns.
I'm thirty-nine I'm seven.
Far down the yard
my father and a neighbor
sail horseshoes through the air.

The clank and settle.

And the past I thought would dwindle
arcs back to me, a hoop.

The men wipe their necks,
the boy walks round the oak:
sometimes our lives rust gently,
a long-handled shovel, leaned
against a sun-warmed wall.

2.

Fourteen, I perch on the wicker seat
in a nimbus of misery, love's shrimp,
hearing the streetcar's crackle and hiss
as the drugstore turns on its corner.

And what was real? The whipped sparks,
the glove puppets, bobbing, the pocket dreams,
this poem-to-be, my father's wharf
of set belief, the wicker and shellac?

Learning to be imperfect—
that's erudition!

Like coolies in flooded fields,
we wade on our own reflections.

    3.

November bleach and brownout. Acid sky,
falsetto sunlight, wire and fluff of weeds, pods,
bone and paper grass-clumps. The dog bounds off,
stitching the field with her nose. Hound city.

It's thirteen years. Different dog, same field,
and double grief: dull for the slumped president,
stake-sharp for my friend's ripped heart—faint
night-cries in the mansions where we lived.

But the bullet grooves are gone, the first dog's dead,
and here is the field, seedy and full of sameness.
Speech fails, years wrinkle. Dream covers dream

that covered dream. My head starts up a jazz
I never could concoct. I have to grin. On the cold pond
the tinsmith wind is whistling at his work.

One Who Came Back

I can't be sure
why we should want you among us

you with your bruised clothes
your fingers thickened by pity

terror's night watchman, mopping blood
where the books lie stitched with quiet

who stood in the grass near the graves
striking the match of darkness

but I know we seem to need you
the way we do bread or warmth

so I'm out here in the moonlight
pounding nails in your footprints

as if that could make you stay.

The Day Nabokov Died

1.

I looked up from my weeding
and saw a butterfly, coal-black,
floating across Plum Creek. Which facts
are laced with lies: it was another day,
it was a monarch—if it was black
it must have been incinerator fluff.

A black hinge, opening and shutting.

2.

Elsewhere the sunset lights
bonfires in hotel windows, gilds the lake,
picks out false embers where it can:
watch crystal, drinking glass, earring.
"Nabokov," someone calls, "is dead . . ."
What would you give to be in, say, Fialta,
hearing the rhythms of a torpid coast?
Or on the porch at the Enchanted Hunters,
conversing in the shadows with Sirin?
Sneezes, lachrymose sighs. Chuckles and coughs.
When at a loss for words, try waving
one helpless hand before your face.

Walking the dog I saw a hawkmoth too,
big as two hands, resting under a streetlight.

3.

In the skyscraper across the lane
an aproned man sets up his easel
at the window opposite, and cocks his head.

What does he see? A dwarf
mixing a violet powder, a fat
landlady playing Patience, a little girl
brushing a velvet coat, in tears,
three people having sex. In short,
the world. Ourselves. Aren't all of us
some form of Maxwell's Demon,
particle sorters, systems
so self-enclosed they work too well to work?

Grandmaster, slip into your fiction like
Houdini diving through a pocket mirror.
Here's wonder, but no grief. And even so,
you'd not have liked this poem. Wan child
in a sailor suit, man running by
waving a gauzy net, tall fencer, pedant,
Hotelmensch, empty suit of clothes . . .

One exile more. One language still to learn.

Occupational Hazards

Butcher
If I want to go to pieces
I can do that. When I try
to pull myself together
I get sausage.

Bakers
Can't be choosers. Rising
from a white bed, from dreams
of kings, bright cities, buttocks,
to see the moon by daylight.

Tailor
It's not the way the needle
drags the poor thread around.
It's sewing the monster together,
my misshapen son.

Gravediggers
To be the baker's dark opposite,
to dig the anti-cake, to stow
the sinking loaves in the unoven—
then to be dancing on the job!

Woodcutter
Deep in my hands
as far as I can go
the fallen trees
keep ringing.

The Picture Says

1.

That we all die, sometimes
when we are children.

That it would look like sleep
if flesh did not decay.

That we are marble, mottled,
that we are piebald clouds.

That we lie in the long grass,
peaceful, hair a little tangled,

grass like wires, spindles, rims,
grass like crisscross lifelines,

paths of the shooting stars,
arcs on the flecked night sky.

2.

Sound of a backhoe, tractor-chug:
this old man is the pond-digger—

he stands by the water's edge,
on his open palm a pond-snail . . .

he is humming, a kind of bee-speech,
while the child sleeps in the grass,

the water a grainy mirror,
the light, the smoky lilies,

and the sky, filling slowly
with bruise-blue rainclouds.

Jaywalker

His arm leaves a dent in my hood.

He lies on the pavement, smiling
to reassure me.
                    Weeks later
the leak in his brain begins.
I try to imagine his headaches,
the murmuring nurses, the priest.
By then he is dead.

                    •

Twenty-two years. I can't
remember his face or name.
He came from a farm across the river.
We tried to visit his father and mother.

Tonight it's as though
my brakes have failed
and I roll through the hushed sirens
past white faces, past
the weary Night Dispatcher, steering
my old, slow Mercury toward
the figure across the river,
the boy from the empty farmhouse
with his smile, his trick headaches.

I would like to light him a candle.
I would like to bring him a drink of water.

I would like to yield the right of way.
I would like to call across the river.

"It's all right now?" I'd shout.

His head would bob in the wind.

Tool Talk

Put tip of poet through loop. Pull tight.
Call this position B. File flash and sand.
Use adze to strike off wobbly-pump
of Handley Page or Spad. Dry roller stocks,
make notch in carrick bits with extra pick
and fit in spindle bush. Dash for the churn,
dash for the peak. Lakes equal paddles, bridles
are for camels, skies, a harness punch will fix
my son's new watch or fill that ladle in the stable.
Fit pitching chisel into granite crotch: release.
If cannon diagram does not apply, destroy.
Let sun god slide through threading lathe. Tie
lightning rod with thong. Work corks in slots of loom.
Rewind. Let sonnet slide from side to side.

After My Death

1.

It will all go backward. Leaves
that fell in October will float up
and gather in trees for greening.
The fire I built will pull
its smoke back in while the logs
blaze and grow whole. Lost hailstones
will freeze themselves back into beads,
bounce once and rise up in a storm,
and as flowers unwilt and then tighten to buds
and the sun goes back toward where it rose
I will step out through shrinking grass
at one for the first time
with my own breath, the wax
and wane of moon, dewsoak, tidewheel,
the kiss of puddle and star.

2.

It will all go on. Rimefrost, mist;
at the cracked mirror the janitor
will comb his hair and hum, three boys
will build a raft, chalk dust will settle
in blackboard troughs, trucks bump
on the railroad crossing, soft talk in trees,
a girl practicing her fiddle: I know this,
I keep imagining it, or trying, and sometimes
when I try hard, it is a small stone fern
delicate, changeless, heavy in my hand.
And then it weighs nothing
and then it is green
and everything is breathing.

A Lowercase Alphabet

a   snail going up the wall

b   hang up the little dipper

c   mouth, moon, riverbend

d   the dipper in the mirror

e   tiny eye of the whale

f   oil well, skate, old pistol

g   what did you do to your glasses?

h   a chimney for every hut

i   the levitation of the spot

j   landscape with fishhook and planet

k   where three roads almost meet

l   romance of the periscope

m   comb from the iron age

n   the hut that lost its chimney

o   simplification of the blood

p   the dipper dead and buried

q   its mirror buried with it

r   geyser that goes off crooked

s   little black love seat

t   the portable cross

u   cross section of a trough

v   the hawk above the valley

w   a graph for winter, pigsfoot

x   dancer, hourglass, black suspenders

y   the root begins to sprout

z   path of the rabbit

The Fool's Tale

When I said good night to the old gaffer
he suddenly flew away laughing!

In the woods I came on a blood-red boar
and a burnt hunter, locked in a stare,

as at Christmas when animals fell on their knees
while the nail and the hammer told them lies.

Magic! So much! You clutch your poor head,
a barrel of rainberries falls from a cloud,

a dwarf whose face is covered with fur
steals your watch, purse, and painted guitar

and a very great darkness covers the earth,
thunder and lightning live at your hearth . . .

No! Hush! It's gone absolutely still—
the stone drops forever into the well,

and a sly little girl with a hood and a muff
walks down the road with a timber wolf.

from The Names of a Hare in English

Les nouns de un levre en Engleis

The man that the hare i-met
Ne shal him nevere be the bet,
Bot if he lei down on londe
That he bereth in his honde,
(Be hit staf, be hit bouwe),
and blesce him with his helbowe.
And mid wel goed devosioun
He shall saien on oreisoun
In the worshipe of the hare
Thenne mai he wel fare.

"The hare, the scotart,
The bigge, the bouchart,
The scotewine, the skikart,
The turpin, the tirart,
The wei-betere, the ballart,
The go-bi-dich, the soillart,
The wimount, the babbart,
The stele-awai, the momelart,
The evil-i-met, the babbart,
The scot, the deubert,
The gras-bitere, the goibert,
The late-at-hom, the swikebert,
The frendlese, the wodecat,
The brodlokere, the bromcat,
The purblinde, the fursecat,
The louting, the westlokere,
The waldenlie, the sid-lokere,
And eke the roulekere;
The stobhert, the long-here,
The strau-der, the lekere

The wilde der, the lepere
The shorte der, the lorkere,
The wint-swift, the sculkere,
The hare serd, the heg-roukere,
The deudinge, the deu-hoppere,
The fitelfoot, the foldsittere,
The ligtt-fot, the fernsittere,
The cawel-hert, the wortcroppere,
The go-bi-ground, the sitte-stille,
The pintail, the toure-tohulle;
The cove-arise,
The make-agrise,
The wite-wombe,
The go-mit-lombe,
The choumbe, the chaulart,
The chiche, the couart,
The make-fare, the breke-forwart,
The fnattart, the pollart,
(His hei nome is srewart);
The hert with the letherene hornes,
The der that woneth in the cornes,
The der that all men scornes,
The der that no-mon ne-dar nemmen."

When thou havest al this i-said,
Thenne is the hare migtt alaid.
Thenne migtt thou wenden forth,
Est and west, and south and north,
Wedrewardes so mon wile,
The man that con ani skile.
Have nou godne dai, sire hare!
God the lete so wel fare,
That thou come to me ded,
Other in cive, other in bred! Amen!
—MS DIGBY 86F 168V. (1272–1283)

1.

Just an old poem-charm. Beyond us,
worn as a bone—but this one
seems to keep doubling back.
Look: fresh tracks, a crosspath. Nervous,
I glance around, I want to know
who wrote it? What liar would claim
seventy-some names for
the pop-eyed, great-hearted
cousin of the rabbit?

I think I know what happened.
I get these fits myself.
For a moment language is everything,
a path to the heart, a small
city of stars on the tongue:
then everything looks in the mirror
and sees his cool twin nothing . . .
seventy names are none.

2.

In the time before dawn, in graylight,
a fur purse hops through the soaked grass,
a stump stands by a stump and then is gone;
this is the time when names are none and many,
the time when names themselves have names.

Say the word, things happen.
Say the long hare is a deer, there's
a crash in the bracken. Say
"Fiddlefoot," you hear pounding
on the packed door of the earth.

Prospero stands in his sour ring,
somebody else's fict. "Turpin,"

he whispers, and a small
furzecat appears at his feet.
"Dewbert," he says, and now
there are two, sidelookers,
late-at-homes, the master smiles,
says "Budget," there are four,
says "Hedgecroucher" and
there are eight but
you know how this
story comes out . . .

What do we have for animal magic
but names, our mumbled spells and charms,
baskets of epithets spilled down the page?

A straw deer stood here
right at this line
but a grassbiter ate it
and then a broomcat swept it away
a windswift blew or flew to where
the westlooker stood looking east
toward the wastelooker in his hair
shirt, but
you know how this goes
you turn the corner of the line
and startle a fernsitter who evaporates
now you see him now
you don't now you name him now . . .

  3.
Along the Vermilion River
the farmer's wife points out some shallow caves
where slaves hid on the way to Canada
and Indians rested, migrating south.
Settlers stood on the bank and watched,

I figure, as I do, hands in my pockets,
wanting to belong to this, or it to me.

An old woman with us knows
the name of every plant.
"What's this?" I ask, testing her.
"Mary's Bedstraw," she says!
I'm shivering. To know the name,
to possess and be possessed!
Don't apologize. Wild Geranium, Dog Violet,
Sneezewort, Bloodroot, Jack-in-the-Pulpit.
So we trail through the river-bottom woods
And names bind us to strange forms of life.
A good new name, I tell myself,
is what the framer feels, turning
an arrowhead or axhead up.
His hand closes around the past,
the mystery of why he's here;
the world extends too far
and yet he's in it, holding a small rock!

We pace on through the woods. Trillium everywhere,
stars on a green spring evening,
bones in an Irish pasture.

   5.
We have some quiet families in this neighborhood.
Constellations, let's start from there. Bear, Plough,
Charles's Wain, how choose? Pleiades, better
as Seven Sisters, but I like Hen and Chickens best.
Is that Pandora, lid-lifting? No, President Taft,
strolling with his cigar. Andromeda,
chained lady? How about Rita Hayworth's
Iceboat? Go on, make up your own,
holding a child's hand, saying: See, there's Moth.

Glove. Submarine. Malcolm's X.
Chandelier. Cottontail. Moebius' Strip: God's Ring.

Well, drop your head.
The field's still here, with its milk vetch and thistles,
the house with its one lamp lit.

   8.
I look at the backs of my hands and get lost:
an old wind bends the grass, blue trails fan
from wrist to flushed and cross-hatched knuckles;
stand on one, look out along
the five peninsulas, ridges crossed
by ravelins and runnels, at the tips
the slick nails flaring; you could do
a tap dance, smiling, and fall off . . .

I look at my hands, searching for their names,
picker and stealer, Guildenstern and Rosencrantz,
the scarred serf who dropped the crystal goblets,
the oldest cups, the simplest maps,
furrow-makers, strangling-partners, fist and claw,
smoothing the child's hair, poking shadows,
wringing laundry, helpless in sleep. I look
at my hands. How could they have names?

   11.
It got away again:

"the deer with the leathery horns
the deer that lives in the corns
the deer that all men scorns
the deer that no one dares to name"

Names, get between me and the things I fear.
Names, for Godsake tell me who I am.

Nothing and everything. The time comes
when you shut the door, step off the porch
and walk across the fields without a word.

12.
A day swings past. A husk of hares
disappears over the hill. Dawn again.
I've looked at the small change in my pocket:
eye, star, hand, rain,
father, mirror, bedstraw, bloodroot.
Now, doing my act, I find a bone,
step in the sour circle, find
the bone knows how to sing:

> *Fowles in the frith*
>   *The fisses in the flod,*
> *And I mon waxe wod.*
>   *Mulch sorwe I walk with*
> *For best of bon and blood.*

Fishes in the flood, and I could go mad:
language, that burrow, warren, camouflage,
language will deceive you and survive you.

Well, then, so what?
I look up *frith*.

Oh game preserve of words!
Oh goldfinch feeding in the buttonbush!
The dogs of death are loosed
upon that little rabbit, Metaphor,
but he can double back. And does.

from

Foraging

But nature is a stranger yet;
The ones that cite her most
Have never passed her haunted house,
Nor simplified her ghost.

To pity those that know her not
Is helped by the regret
That those who know her, know her less
The nearer her they get.

—EMILY DICKINSON

In My Own Back Yard

1.

July, I'm dozing in sun on the deck,
one thrush is singing among the high trees,
and Li Po walks by chanting a poem!
He is drunk, he smells unwashed.
I can see tiny lice in his hair
and right through him
a brown leaf in the yard
flips over flips,
again lies still,
all this time
no wind.

2.

From behind November glass I watch the wind
truck all its winter furnishings
item by item into my yard.
In a dusty raincoat my neighbor
throws a tennis ball, over and over,
to exercise his police dog.

Sometimes I feel like one of the world's bad headaches,
sometimes I think I get no closer
to what I have wanted to mean
than the gumshoe calling
"Testing"
up to the bugged ceiling . . .

You can try to put words to a mood
or tell yourself to ignore it,
but what kind of message is coming
from the chickadee, dapper

in his black mask and skullcap,
grooming himself on the big pine's branch-tip?

His music is small and monotonous,
but it's his own.

3.
I am turning pages in lamplight.
Outside, above blue snow, in February dusk,
in the double world of glass,
more pages flip, like wings—
this merging of me and the world
done with mirrors and windows.

4.
Hunting for duck eggs at the end of March
I watch three mallards and a speckled female make
a tight flotilla on the swollen creek.

The dog barks at her counterpart
on the other bank. Nothing is green
the way these mallards' heads are green.

Empty-handed, I turn back to the house.
Small waterlights
play on the underbranches of the ash. High up
the sycamore lifts its light-peeled limbs
against a turning sky.

5.
Late May. Summer coming on again. I think
Li Po may not be back. Worried about
the world's end, as, I realize,
I have been most of my life,

I take my work outside
and sit on the deck, distracted.
It was a day like this, I think,
in Hiroshima.
Distracted.
There must be something in the pinecones
that the chickadees— There's another one.
What's this that's snowing down? Husks, pollen,
freckle-sized petals from our wild cherry trees!

We sneeze and plant tomatoes. Ultimatums. The world
comes close and goes away
in rhythms that our years
help us begin to understand.

We haven't long to live.
And the world? Surely the world . . .
A deep breath. Sunshine.
Mosquitoes, bird calls, petal-hail.

A Ghost, to One Alive

There you sit, in the midst of your heart's rich tick,
your breath coming and going,
a lax and happy piston;

your eyes blink, your tongue slicks your lips,
your brain hums, gobbling oxygen.
Oh hot, unconscious life . . .

I know I am hard to imagine—
a smoke bag, a spindle of mist, fume of an old fear-pot—
but you are just the opposite:

you ruin this sweet hush, two times too real,
and I find I have to drift back
from your clicks, wheezes, and smells,

your mask of hope over a hopeless gape,
one eye on the wagging clock, muffled
amazement, bundle of hungers, oven stuffed with yourself!

If you knew a bit more you might envy me,
moon-scalded as I am,
voodoo-hooded and vague as cheesecloth,

a simulacrum of solid old you,
the last billow from a cold, closed furnace,
a dimple, at best, in existence,

the bird call without the bird.

Mesa Verde

1.
Drive up with me.

Show the way, magpie, across the invisible bridge.

Old ghosts, be near
but not too near.

September, early morning, not a trace of haze.
Rabbitbrush glows like sulphur
and the mesa dozes in sunlight.
The corner-eye specter on the trail
is a rock or a pinyon stump
or a tourist aiming a camera.
Sun-shimmer and squint. The gorges
lie silent and waterless
like dreams of river valleys
that rivers never made.

Climb into me, Anasazi,
take my tongue and language,
tell how you came to farm the corn,
hoarding the snowmelt, learned
to be weavers, potters, masons
in the huge American daylight,
gathering pine nuts, hunting mule deer,
crushed juniper berries with water,
mixed them in cornmeal for our thick blue bread
—what was our word for bread?—
and praised the gods, hunched in our smoky kivas
singing over the soul-hole
the mystery of our birth

when first a man crawled out
from warm dark to open air.

We farmed till the droughts got worse,
the corn and squash and beans
shriveled and died, the game thinned out,
and we moved down to live
in the scoops and pockets of cliffs
where water seeped and food could be hoarded,
two hundred feet below the dizzy rim,
nine hundred feet above the canyon floor
perching like squirrels and jays
because the gods decided
(what were the names of the gods?)
that life had been too easy,
that snows should stop and water shrink
and we too nest against the canyon walls
mindful of hardship.

   2.
Silence again. Silence in Spruce Tree Lodge,
at Hovenweep, Chaco Canyon,
stone and sunlight resting against each other
and no ghosts coming to converse
at nightfall when the stars spring out
and we stand on the rimrock, staring up
at the Bear and the hunters chasing him,
at the stocky women, grinding corn
among dogs, turkeys, children,
while smoke floats from the kiva
and snow-fluff crowns the sagebrush.

Silence, solstice to equinox.
Empty granaries, old firepits, dry cisterns.
The sun walks through the canyon,

peering under the sandstone overhangs,
and the wind walks too, wearing pine-smell.
Skull-jar and serviceberry,
sipapu and alcove,
a ghostly sea of buffalo,
tossing on the plains below.

And the light slips off
among the rifted mesas,
the dead are wrapped in turkey-feather blankets,
rabbit-fur robes, yucca mats,
and buried in the trashpiles,
while the living move south or west
in search of food and water
leaving it all to the sun and wind and stars
who lived here first.

The night is dreamless,
a star chart, a crescent-wrench moon,
and the air hangs quietly
a sea whose bottom you walk
looking up through the empty miles,
the rocks around you like turned backs.

The sun cracks earth, the frost splits rocks.
What's history if it falls away,
if the brick-colored woman
milling corn in the courtyard
isn't kin, can't leave us this landscape,
neighbor horizon and brother canyon wren,
toehold and rampart,
the old river of belief
that pounds through empty gullies
like sunlight and moonlight
leaving them undisturbed.

Touch me. Moisten my mouth,
dazzle my eyes. Link me a moment to the life
that wore on gently here
and left these ruins to the sun.

3.
In the swept museum,
smaller than hummingbirds
these people kneel and climb in little models
weaving their tiny baskets
hoarding their dollhouse ears of corn.

And who doesn't crouch below some diorama
while sunlight moves across a mesa,
hearing the call of raven,
glimpsing the Steller's jay?

I write this on an overhang, a porch,
against a California canyon
that runs down to the sea;
across the way the houses perch and nestle
among the live oaks, palms, and avocado trees.
Hummingbirds float through my eucalyptus
like strange little fingers, or gods,
and the raven's shadow travels the rough slope,
wrinkling and stretching,
recollection of another life.

The hummingbird comes to rest, midair,
and the mind meshes with other minds,
lost patterns of thought that hang
over the mesas, across the hillsides,
in pools of light and shadow,
and make us bow in thought or prayer,
silence or speech,

while the sun that walked this canyon
when it was brown and empty
and will have it so again
carries the day away
through dry and shining air.

Laguna Beach, September 1981

October Couplets

1.

Again the cold: shot bolt, blue shackle,
oxalic acid, bleaching a rubber cuff,

a cow-eyed giantess, burning roots and brush,
the streak and smash of clouds, loud settling jays,

crows roosting closer—my older-by-one-year bones
have their own dull hum, a blues: it's all plod,

but they want to go on, above timberline,
to boulders, florets, ozone, then go free

in the old mill that the wind and the frost run
all day all night under the gauze and gaze of stars.

2.

Somewhere between sperm cell and clam shell
this space cruiser takes me places I'd rather

stay clear of: a planet all graveyard, mowed,
graveled and paved, bride-light and parson-shade,

or a milkweed, bitter, about to burst, or a dropped
acorn even a squirrel didn't want, browning to black,

and I have to learn to relax with it all, to sing
"Where the bee sucks, there suck I," though the lily

is sticky and choking, bees don't suck, and the sting
is a greeting you never recover from.

3.
"Steam of consciousness," a student's fluke,
makes me see a lake, linen-white at evening,

some amnesia-happy poet all curled up
sucking a rock at its black bottom;

oblivion tempts everyone, but I
would miss too much—whales and ticks,

the weather's subtle bustle, blue-crab clouds,
my kite rising, paper and sticks, a silver ember,

while the poem's ghost waits by the empty band shell,
does a little tango, taps out its own last line.

4.
But this fall rain, somehow both thread and button,
sewing itself to the malachite grass,

beading the clubs and brushes of the spruce—
all day I have sat as if gazing over water,

wind feathering the reservoir, stupid as a church,
and thought of summer: all those burst horizons,

mineral cities, rosy meat, clean seas, and shaggy islands,
the wine cork popping in the grape arbor,

these things seem better and clearer than gods just now,
raspberries hung like lamps among their brambles.

5.

These leaves, these paper cutouts drifting my yard,
stars, fish, mitten, saddles: the badges and epaulets

of emptiness—last night in my dream
I was the killer, the guard who failed to stop him,

and the child who froze and was spared. Nothing lasts,
sang the crowd, and I answered, It sure does;

Is nothing sacred, roared the statesman—I do
believe it is, said I . . . I wake and shave,

still full of my dreamflood—oh skim-milk sky,
oh brown star curling in my hand . . .

Basho

Tonight, on the other side of the lake,
someone is walking with a lantern.

The changing light on the water
—a blossom, a wasp, a blowfish—
calls me back from desolation
and makes me sigh with pleasure.

How can I be so foolish?

•

It's true! All night
I listen to the rain
dripping in a basin . . .
in the morning I have a haiku.
So what!

All these years
And I think I know
just about nothing:
a close-grained man
standing in haze by the warm lake
hearing the slap of oars
and sobbing.

•

For weeks now, month, a year,
I have been living here at Unreal Hut
trying to decide what delight means
and what to do with my loneliness.

Wearing a black robe,
Weaving around like a bat . . .

•

Fallen persimmon, shriveled chestnut,
I see myself too clearly.

A poet named for a banana tree!

Some lines of my own come back:
Year after year
on the monkey's face—
a monkey mask.

I suppose I know what I want:
the calm of a wooden Buddha,
the state of mind of that monk
who forgot about the snow
even as he was sweeping it!

But I can't run away from the world.
I sit and stare for hours at
A broken pot or a bruised peach.
An owl's call makes me dance.

I remember a renga we wrote
that had some lines by Boncho:
somebody dusts the ashes
from a grilled sardine . . .
And that's the poem! That sardine!
And when it is, I feel
it is the whole world too.

But what does it mean
and how can it save you?

When my hut burned down
I stood there thinking,
"Homeless, we're all of us homeless . . ."

Or all my travels, just so much
slogging around in the mire,
and all those haiku,
squiggles of light in the water . . .

•

Poems change nothing, save nothing.

Should the pupil love
the blows of the teacher?

A storm is passing over.
Lightning, reflected in the lake,
scares me and leaves me speechless.

I can't turn away from the world
but I can go lightly . . .

Along the way small things
may still distract me:
a crescent moon, a farmer
digging for wild potatoes,
red-pepper pods, a snapped chrysanthemum . . .

Love the teacher, hate the blows.

Standing in mist by the shore,
nothing much on my mind . . .

•

Wearing a black robe,
weaving around like a bat—

or crossing a wide field
wearing a cypress hat!

Six Ghosts

THE SUICIDE

You think I opened this door
on an impulse. I wish that were true.
But the door was there all my life.
Even when I looked away
I could feel its cold outline.
It knew. Knew I would touch the strange handle,
take one last breath, swing it ajar,
enter that room
empty of me.

THE HUNTER

The deer that had bedded down
in the second growth by the creek
started up and was gone
before my eyes and ears
could take it in.

Now, among mind-shaped trees,
I run ahead of the deer when I want to.

THE SAILOR

If I come back to the moment of my death,
the ship coasting across black water,
its sails half-furled, glowing white,
and the storm looming beyond—

If I come back it is not regret
but because I am part of some huge dance
that takes me there, breathless and laughing.

THE SIMPLETON

Soap and the moon and my crown askew.

THE POET

All of the words cracked open
and I hatched out
to the world I used to watch
from the distance of my head:
thunder-scrubbed rainbows,
ploughed fields like rosy cocoa dust,
and that voice, echoing behind me.

THE READER

Now that my life is a cool book
I have read once, I can come back
to browse. Often I turn
to a chapter where nothing happened.
Even that is unbearably full,
and I stare at a single page for days,
its strange marks, its wild white silence.

The Self: A Sonnet Sequence

1.
If we are what we see, hear, handle,
then I am London now: rainlight and chimneypots,
shuddering buses, streaky-bacon flatblocks,
rooks in a queue. Reading your novel, I was a girl

who took up living in a barn. Sense-pestered,
trailing itself around the world,
the self is now and then complete as it looks in
to mingle with an afternoon, a page, a person . . .

In the Siberian frozen tombs they found
wool socks, expressive faces, rugs, fresh leather,
a chieftain's arm still glowing with tattoos:

what the self freezes, what the self digs up—
what do you want to call it, kid?
Weather. A city on a page. A mirror.

2.
Self as imperialist, pushing out his borders?
Oh, the ego rides in armor, bellows threats,
but his helmet's a pocked kettle, he'll turn tail
as soon as he sees the torches of the future,

he's far less real than, say, his horse's shoulder.
The anarchists he hired are dismantling
what's left of his soft palace, heaving chunks
into the soft and unbecoming river.

A candle: what it means to do is vanish,
brightly. The self: what it means to do
is make a candle. Something of that kind,

and the object—horseshoe, cabbage, poem—
is what the self just hoped to run together to
and fill: a cup of anonymity.

3.
Well, no, not run together. Scatter: smoke
in its eloquent hoods and cowls. Clouds,
their race and rain. We're swarms of funny matter
(ice, rust, grasses, moonsparks, puff-paste)

longing and fearing to disperse. "Can't get away
from you-know-who" (scratched on a mirror), but the eye
sees way beyond the eye, and the mooncalf mind
sits on its shelf and flies great kites.

"After the dancers have left
and the grand ballroom is empty,
the old beekeeper brings

a rustling and humming box;
and the band begins to play again,
but you've never heard the music."

4.
My young self comes to see me, fresh and friendly.
He is from 1957, and anxious to get back.
I think he is just polite about my acting
as though we had lots in common. Stands in the doorway,

charming but rushed. I'm amazed
that I like him so much, like him at *all*,
he has such an air of self-discovery,
as if one day to the next he *knows* himself

(first love, acting, superficial poems),
a life he thinks I'm merely interrupting.
I live inside his dream, he inside mine,

and we back away from each other, smiling,
a couple of meadows, a couple of knives,
affection brimming between us as we go.

5.
Is a pebble. Is a bubble. Drags its little sled
through empty salt flats under a cobalt sky
of nailed-up stars. Is a lamb with real sharp teeth,
a tongue waltzing in a moonlit clearing. Is

a donkey, leaning against a mulberry tree
in which the silkworms spin their mysteries;
hugs itself, hugs itself and cries,
a horn full of sparks, a shadow at a keyhole.

The critic wanted to enter the very brush stroke,
then find the brush, then climb the painter's arm,
muscle and vein and nerve to mind and heart:

instead he stumbled and then he was falling forever
through meaningless words that were falling too
in exactly the opposite direction.

6.

Has its parents strapped on like backpacks,
grandparents in a suitcase; its orders are
to move the grand piano over a mountain
without upsetting the buckets of milk for its children.

The house is sheared open by the wrecking ball
and there is the bathroom, flashing its mirror,
the wallpaper, losing track of its pattern,
the chest of drawers where father kept his condoms.

Tear rolling down the hill of the corpse's
cheek. Big tear that rolls off the stiff blue chin.
Things left behind, trashbin and junkyard.

Rain won't be different from skin.
Eye won't be different from view.
Smoke will take root and every flower float.

7.

Hyde, this is Jekyll: no more rages,
no more rapes and stranglings. I leave this flat
only for necessary shopping.
On the horizon, the orphanage burns.

Evelyn Waugh, timid of ridicule,
built up a carapace so thick
he could hardly move inside it—except to write
painful, hilarious novels, ridiculing the world.

The daylight brightens, dims, and brightens.
Late March. Atoms of nostalgia,
flakes of essential self. Crusoe on his beach

pondering a footprint. Still March. Outside
the blown rain writes nonsense on the windows,
the pear tree strains against its ivory buds.

8.
One of those houses where the eyes of portraits move
and suits of armor mutter by the stairs.
But this was worse. The chairs had body-heat
and every sink was specked with blood.

I swept from room to room, my cape
billowing out behind. Sat by the fire
poking the panting coals. Hid beneath a bed
and listened to them screwing in the attic.

Think of a liquid. Dog slobber. Cattle drool.
Dipped up in a leaf-cup from a spring. It's true,
anything other than human could comfort me now

like that French poet who could put his face
against a hanging side of beef
and still his fear.

9.
Goodbye to the night sky, the Milky Way
a bone-seam on a cranium, vein in a cave.
Now dawn is a rooster, noon a pheasant
crossing the road. I drive. Land's End, Tintagel,

the landscape fills me slowly, like a sail.
A daylight display, a wind off the Atlantic,
ego shadows sailing across pieced fields,
a herd of clouds without a shepherd.

Sometimes the world will fit you like a sweater
and you think ingenuity and fortitude
can see you through, your recipe and axis.

I have to say this clumsily; at best,
the image trembles in its instant, star
in a pail of water carried through a glade.

    10.

In Voronezh did Mandelstam
sing of his death the winter I was born
in Davenport, in Iowa, all mother's milk and love
against his sour tea and fear. The contrast

makes me wince. I want . . . to be a goldfinch too?
No, and I'm not the point. Nor Mandelstam. We're both
exhibits of the self, the flesh made word,
singing its own confusion and delight:

all this takes place despite the big world's Stalins.
I write this in The Royal Mail, in Islington.
"Hullo, Stanley," says the barmaid. Pool balls click,

the jukebox throbs. We bob on currents,
taking the world as best we can, each planet
cruising its dawns and dusks around the sun.

England. January–May 1979

Hunting for Mushrooms in Orange County

Like a snail on a cabbage leaf
I move along this hillside.

Blank eyeballs bulging in the grass,
doorknobs to darkness, night's white knuckles
the scattered cups and saucers of the dead,
old smoky hard-ons coaxed up by the rain!

There are stars and flowers in this world,
green sprouts, plump nuts, threshed grain,
fruit in bright rinds and clusters—

but there are these buttons too,
these pallid lamps, lit by a secret,
tokens so strange we hold our breath to eat them,
puffball, campestris, morel,
wrinkled and chalky blebs of foam.

I look up from my gathering
and think I don't know where I am . . .
the buckskin hills, the instant cities,
this grainy earth we find and lose
and find again
and learn to say we shall lie down in,

meanwhile nibbling on these swollen caps,
beautiful messages of decay, from roots, bones, teeth,
from coal and bark, humus and pulp and sperm,

muzzle-skull, channel and hand, the all-containing dead,
invisible branchings of our living smolder—
I glance around me, half-bewildered,
here in this California sunlight,
spore-dust drifting right through my body

a meadow-mushroom humming between my fingers.

Elegy in the Form of an Invitation

JAMES WRIGHT, *b. 1927, Martins Ferry, Ohio;*
d. 1980, New York City

Early spring in Ohio. Lines
of thunderstorms, quiet flares
on the southern horizon.
A doctor stares at his hands.
His friend the schoolmaster
plays helplessly with a thread.

I know you have put your voice aside
and entered something else.

I like to think you could come back here now
like a man returning to his body
after a long dream of pain and terror.

It wouldn't all be easy:
sometimes the wind blows birds
right off their wires and branches,
chemical wastes smolder on weedy sidings,
codgers and crones still starve in shacks
in the hills above Portsmouth and Welfare . . .
hobo, cathouse, slagheap, old mines
that never exhaust their veins—
it is all the way you said.

But there is this fierce green
and bean shoots poking through potting soil
and in a month or so the bees
will move like sparks among the roses.

And I like to think
the things that hurt won't hurt you any more
and that you will come back
in the spring, for the quiet,
the dark shine of grackles,
raccoon tracks by the river,
the moon's ghost in the afternoon,
and the black earth behind the ploughing.

Vermont Summer: Three Snapshots, One Letter

In this picture I am standing in a meadow,
holding a list of fifty-one wildflowers.
It is Vermont, midsummer, clear morning
all the way to the Adirondacks.
I am, as usual, lost. But happy,
shaggy with dew. Waving my list.
The wind that blows the clouds across these mountains
has blown my ghosts away, and the sun
has flooded my world to the blinding-point.
There's nothing to do till galaxy-rise
but name and gather the wildflowers.
This is called "pearly everlasting."
And this one is arrow-leaved tearthumb!
Hawkweed, stitchwort, dogbane, meadow-rue . . .
The dark comes on, the fireflies weave around me,
pearl and phosphor in the windy dark,
and still I am clutching my list,
saying "hop clover, fireweed, cinquefoil,"
as the Milky Way spreads like an anchor overhead.

ROBERT FROST'S CABIN

He perched up here at the lip of the woods
summer after summer. Grafted his apple trees
into a state of confusion. Came down
two or three times a season to be lionized.
Mesmerized visitors with talk,
or hid from them. Or both.

Charles and I look in his windows.
There's his famous chair.
The place is tiny, but the view is good.
We shake our heads at his solitude.
Couldn't he have the kind of friendship
that brought us here together?

How can we keep from becoming such mollusks?
Easy, says Charles. Don't live that long.

HAY-HENGE

After the meadow was mowed and before
the bales were gathered, the students
erected a midget Stonehenge in the moonlight.
It stood there all the next day:
real from a distance, and up close
sweet-smelling and short-lived.

Off and on I've been pondering models:
I think they are all we have.
Snapshots, cabins, lists. Metonymies.
At Lascaux they've opened
a replica of the caves. *I will get
Peter Quince to write a ballad of this dream . . .*
The sun goes down beyond Hay-Henge;
clouds and mountains mix in the distance.

LETTER TO CHLOE

Since you left, we've had
wild blackberries, northern lights,
and one grand thunderstorm.
Again, these mountains have been

Chinese with their graduated mist.
Tonight it's clear and we hope to see
a meteor shower. I'm teaching Vaughan,
who tried to show us another world
with images of light, and knew
he needed dark to make the light more real.

I shake my head, still lost.
I'm lucky if I find a berry,
name a flower, see a shooting star.
You and I cried a little at the airport:
each parting's a model for something bigger.
But I don't think the models mean much.
We try to take them as they come:
A trefoil in the hand, a meteor trail
crossing the retina, a black and glinting
tart-sweet berry in the mouth.

Three Walks

A path, garden, a country lane,
with a very old lady and her daughter,
the whole evening holding tremulous
as though it might never end.
A codger watering his broccoli
talks up the art of gardening as
we gaze at his cabbages and gooseberries.
By his garden wall and along the lane
foxglove is speechlessly in bloom,
herb Robert, hogweed, eglantine,
everything, even the grass and cuckoo-spittle,
touched with the slow welling-up of life.
When we come back I hear again
some thrush in the deep shade
making a music as intricate
as what we were walking through.

NEAR ARCIDOSSO, TUSCANY. JULY 1979

Maybe I like this city for being
nearly unknown, off in the mountains.
Over and over the cuckoo calls from the chestnuts
this sleepy midday. Red-and-lemon posters
for a circus, Orfei, plaster every wall,
and I can imagine a humdrum Orpheus
ambling the narrow street to the bakery,
pausing to stare
at the round fountain where a stone mask

blows a thin rope of water
into a basin, a rope without ends.
He would climb to the old castle,
baking in sunshine, where
the air is alive with bees
that build in the crumbling masonry.
What would he make of it all? Would he stand,
his eyes blurring with tears,
looking back through the smoke of time
at the women and men, come and gone,
who have seen how the earth is lovely
and seen how its meanings desert them?

NEAR LORAIN AND OBERLIN, OHIO. JULY 1982

Backward and forward in time, as if
by way of England and Italy, I've come
to stand in the Kmart parking lot
while Cassiopeia hangs askew
beyond the cornfields, come to hear doves
calling all morning in the rain
like very tired cuckoos.
Tomorrow, the Fourth of July, I'll go
mushroom-gathering in the cemetery
to the rumble of summer thunder
among the distant dead, Huron Weed, Amanda Peabody,
and the newer dead I knew, George Lanyi, Jean Tufts,
and if it's not so time-caressed
still I will pause there, startled,
as though I stood on my own heart
in nature's haunted house,
as again, in the long-drawn evening,
with the fireflies signaling—

commas, hyphens, exclamation marks—
and the skyrockets in the distance—
foxgloves, fountains, bees,
constellations and mushrooms
hung for a second or two
on the dim sky above the trees.

from

Earthshine

The Moon-Globe

This small tin model of the moon,
gift of a friend, tipped on its stand
is one of the featured and featureless
things that survive you now.

It's mapped, but not in relief:
one can see and study, but not feel,
the craters and mountain ranges.
Sometimes I rub the missing wrinkles.

There's no dark side to this moon.
No light one either.
Just enough gloss to reflect
a smudge of daylight on its gray-blue surface.

I move it from desk to bedside,
giving my grief a little spin,
putting the surface, which ought to be rough,
against my shaved and moony cheek.

Nine Deaths

"Cancer is a series of deaths."
—GEORGIA NEWMAN

1. SURGERY

Late April. You've just learned
They will cut away your breast, or part of it.

We've cried,
discussed statistics,
told our children and friends. For relief
and a little privacy
we drive out
to West Road
south of the reservoir,
and walk in the green spring evening
hearing cows and birds, watching leafing trees.

"The world's so beautiful," I say. Or is that you?
We hold hands.
This is a death, the first,
and we can bear it.

Not too bad.
Not good, though.

2. LIVER SCAN

It's summer now. Your radiation's over
and you're to start
chemotherapy:
"poisoning the body
to poison the disease," in one view,

but a way to buy some time and hope for most.
In the last conference at the Cleveland Clinic
before we leave for six weeks in Vermont
we get bad news:
a liver scan
shows two spots,
metastases,
the cancer erupting in a new place.

The chemo will have to be
much more severe: you'll have nausea, fatigue,
you'll lose your lovely hair.
I hold your hand
tightly
as the doctor talks.
We both feared this.
The statistics he gives
are still encouraging
but hope has shrunk.
This is another death. We live
inside a tighter circle now.

All day we drive east.
Since Margaret, with us,
doesn't know and you don't want to worry her,
nothing is said.
Whenever I glance at you
your face is peaceful.
We listen to music, read the scenery,
fold and unfold our maps.
Oh this is a death, all right,
as we head up
toward the Green Mountains
clinging to two hopes:
recovery, hardly likely,
and a good long stand-off in your body

between the cancer and the chemicals
that will start to weaken your heart.

You have
a little more
than nineteen months
to live.

3.   INDEFINITELY

Now there's an interlude of nearly a year
in which there's no death, just some dying,
and most of it is bearable.
Vermont is peaceful. Bread Loaf is lively
in just the right way. We go to Burlington
for treatments, shop for a wig,
bring back fresh bagels.
Walks, reading, visits from friends,
at our small cabin in the woods.
You audit a course on *Ulysses,*
work on an article, your last one.
We don't have sex as often—
you feel fragile and the chemo
makes your vagina dry—
but we feel close and, often, happy,
lucky to have each other for the time,
and our two children, half adults,
one with us, raising a robin in a box,
the other at home with a job,
playing at man of the house.

By the end of the summer you're bald
and we're off for four months in England,
me to teach, you to research and write
and visit museums as you can.

You're not as able as you hoped.
Everywhere in the city
you need to take my arm,
shaky in traffic and crowds,
tiring easily.

You stay home a lot and read.
You hate the wig and tend to wear
scarves and bandannas,
whose look, peasant or gypsy, I grow to love.
We get to a lot of theater,
exhibits, side trips to Bath, Stratford,
the Lake District.
Sometimes your appetite is good,
sometimes you can't take much
except some tea and oatmeal.
Sometimes you throw up, again and again.

We know it's the price we pay
for holding off the disease
and you don't complain.

You don't complain about London either
but I can tell
how glad you are
to get back home.

Now they change the regimen.
After a year, people on this one
start to have massive heart failure.

You ask your Cleveland doctor
how long you'll be on this new set of drugs.
As long as they work, he tells you,
to keep those liver spots from spreading.
And then? And then a new set.

And how long on chemotherapy?
Indefinitely, he says.

It comes across us both,
a sickening dawn that we saw coming:
we can't expect to beat the disease.
It's June. Ripe summer has set in again.
This is a death.

4. SEIZURE

One August night, after a bad movie
(Indiana Jones and the Temple of Doom),
you wake me with your movements.
Thinking you need to go to the bathroom,
I try to help you up, but you fall, helpless,
hitting your face on the night table.
Then come convulsions. Then unconsciousness.
Is this a stroke? Some new disease?
Shaking, I summon the ambulance
and they take you to Emergency.
You have another seizure there. They drug you, admit you,
and send me home at 3 a.m. Next day,
a CAT scan confirms the doctor's hunch:
two little tumors in the brain.
These can be treated by radiation, we're assured.
The real risk continues in the liver.
You can have radiation to the skull and still
help me drive Margaret to college.
Gradually, gingerly,
we move back into our routines.
You have no memory of your seizure.
You often ask me about it.
I remember everything
too vividly: the horror of your fall,

my helplessness, your absence in convulsions
and unconsciousness.
It's taken me three months
to tell this part of the story.
That's how I know what a death it is.
Almost the biggest one.
And yet our lives go on.
You have a new doctor, whom you like the best
of all of them. You're back at work.
Like Indiana Jones you seem to have had
one more miraculous escape.
Down in my heart, I know different.

5.   LUNG SPOTS

September. A chest X-ray
that looked all right at first
is taken again and studied further.
There are two spots on the lung.

This isn't so serious, we're told.
If the spots don't grow, the new chemo's working,
and it will be easier to monitor.
The liver is still
the biggest danger.

Neither one of us, for a while,
can admit to what we're thinking:
now the disease has turned up
four separate places. How long
till it spreads to yet another?
And when it turns up in the blood, the bone,
the other breast . . .

I know how much this sets you back
by how long it takes you to tell
your father and children.

I don't know how much
you cry in the bathroom
or when I'm not around.

This is a little death, but it goes deep.

6. ANEMIA

You keep on going to work.
Morning after morning,
dropping you off,
watching your slow movements,
I feel my heart
crack into contrary parts:
admiration for your courage,
sorrow for your slow decline.

Christmas comes, a loved one,
but you are weak and can't eat much.
You sleep a lot and we both pretend
your lack of appetite is temporary,
a matter of adjusting to the chemo
and learning what is palatable.

Oh eating is death and hunger is death,
and I don't know, or won't admit it.
We drift through January, a rugged month,
and I make soups, brown rice and junket.
Somehow the things you ate as a child,
your mother's bridge-club casseroles
and thirties cooking,

help you most. You dwindle,
and we both try not to notice.
Finally, one early February night,
your breathing grows terribly labored
and next day
I take you to the doctor.

You're anemic, she tells us,
and some blood transfusions will help.
She admits you to the hospital.
I'm relieved
to have you in competent hands.
But there's something ominous in this.
You sense it more than I do.
Mid-afternoon, the last time we talk,
you cry a little. I try to cheer you up
and promise to make the calls
to friends and family
to say you're in the hospital
and hoping to get out
healthy and pink again
in a day or two.

7.   HEART FAILURE

Your heart fails during the transfusion.
Weakened by medication, it can't drive
your damaged lungs.
Your breathing stops.
They rush you to Intensive Care
and manage to revive you,
hooking you up to a breathing machine
that helps you—makes you?—go on living.

You never regain consciousness.
Three days we watch beside your bed,
talking to you, whispering, pleading.
I summon the family,
chat with the minister,
go through the motions of normal life,
try to endure
the pity of watching you kept alive
by a mindless apparatus.

I want to let you go. I want to keep you.

Where has your beauty gone,
your gaze, your poise and animation?
What or who am I standing beside?
What ears hear my whispers of love?

8.   UNPLUG THE RESPIRATOR

This is the doctor's idea.
A scan shows you've probably been gone,
brain-dead,
since the heart first stopped.

Is this then the moment of death?
This is the eighth of nine.

9.   SHE'S LIKE A PAINTING / BLESS HER HEART

At the last you look composed,
unhooked, released, at peace
as we come in groups of two and three
to take our leave of you.

I can touch and kiss you again,
though your waxy stillness
tells me I'm kissing your husk.

My mind shoots like a bobsled
back through the whole course of the illness.
Once again, arm in arm,
summoning courage,
we are walking out of the Cleveland Clinic.

One last look for us.
"She's like a painting," whispers Margaret.
And that is true.

"Bless her heart," says my simple mother,
twice,
and those words are oddly right.
That damaged heart
that kept you going
and gave you strength to face your death . . .

You're like a painting.

Bless your heart.

10. CODA

Your deaths are over.
My dreams begin.

In the first you are wearing a striped blouse
and vomiting in the kitchen sink.
I watch your back from a helpless distance.

In the second, helping you move to a chair
at some social gathering,
I realize you are lifeless
like a mummy or a dummy.

In the third, I arrive running, late,
for some graveside service.
You are waiting in the crowd, impatient and withdrawn.
But then you embrace me.
What a relief to touch you again!

These dreams are not your visits,
just my clumsy inventions.
I live in an empty house
with wilting flowers and spreading memories
and my own heart
that hollows and fills.
I'm addressing you
and you can't hear me.
If you can, you don't need
to be told this story.
I need to tell it to myself
until I can stand to hear it,
which may be never.

And you're not here
except in the vaguest ways.

Were you the hawk
that followed us back
from your memorial service
that brilliant winter day?

Are you the rabbit
I keep seeing
that's tamer than it should be?

I wish I could believe it.
You're none of these things or all of them.

What does Montale say?
Words from the oven, words from the freezer,
that's what poetry is.

This is neither.
This is an empty house and a heart
that hollows and fills, hollows and fills.

Chloe Hamilton Young, 1927–1985

from Poem in Three Parts

To Halley's Comet

Thumbsmear, figment, dust-and-ice-ball portent,
what the Chinese called "broomstar" and the Greeks
named for its gassy hair, a halo of plasma
kinked and knotted by magnetic fields: comet
my father will see twice, I'll offer this to you,
since it deals with gravity, motion and light
and you can mean all three,
                              though you don't know
Earth's lovely pull, only the sun's fierce yo-yo game,
and you can't move, except along your long, looped track,
and you can't see the hues and gleams
our light-show throws around, just your own blue glow
in the proton wind—still, I'd like to mark your passage
by this small celebration, twinned with my own life,
of where we live and why we tend to love it.

1.

What stands on one leg at night?
staggers and stalks?

Oedipus never heard the whole riddle—
the Sphinx held something back . . .

What feels its leg turn to one root
twisting down into humus and duff?

—Even today in modern Thebes
   somebody building a house
   will find in the excavation
   so many statues and funeral pots
   the project turns into a dig—

Oh cities and cities of the dead . . .

What made the Laius family limp?

                                    It's hard
to free your foot from that dreamy earth-pull
and you drag it, leaving a seed-grave.

3.

When Hare first heard about Death
he gnashed his teeth, went to his lodge,
and started screaming.

        My aunts and uncles mustn't die!

His thoughts went up to the cliffs and they started to crumble,
crawled across rocks and they shattered,
went down in the earth where everything stilled and stiffened,
glanced at the sky and birds crashed down, dead thoughts.

He went to his lodge, lay down,
and wrapped himself in his blanket.

> *Earth isn't big enough.*
> *It will be hard, all those dead,*
> *and not enough earth to hold them!*

And he lay there, wrapped in his blanket.

4.

And isn't the earth our goddess?
When we run through a muddy field
don't we step in her clutching hands?

Weren't the male sky-gods
our dream of escape from her? Isn't
gravity
mother-love?
Apron-string, homing instinct?

To deny autochthony!
                        Going up in smoke,
the rising-trick of the kite,
                        the swaddled astronaut
knifing his lifeline and tumbling away
                        into a motherless dark . . .

In a basket
hung from my cruising balloon
I find

my gaze
pulled to her fields
all fenced and winter-fallow.

Today she is sound asleep, it's bitter February,
even the birds have abandoned
this white and star-crossed air,
and I can talk about her some.

I know I touched her at Castlerigg
in cloud-wet Cumberland—
not the stone circle so much
as the barely visible furrows
left by the Dark Age ploughs,
marks of her longevity.

Cremate us! We plead, dreaming escape again, but the smoke
melts into the water cycle, her old prayer wheel, and the ashes,
even dumped at sea,
drift in the currents of her cold and giant love.

5.

Nineteen-oh-five.
Joyce in Trieste
Is writing "The Dead."
Nora and Giorgio are asleep.
Something about Rome,
maybe all those catacombs
or the sleepy look of ruins,
reminded him of Ireland
and its loose hordes of ghosts.

He writes the final sentences
and his Gabriel gives in
to the vast chthonic pull

while Joyce imagines he
himself goes free. Not so.
All Trieste's asleep—
the snow is general
all over Europe.
Joyce had a mother too.

7.

Bat-shadows
hoof prints
"pool and rut peel parches"

all her marks and mottles

the garden, the lawn, the tennis court, lawn again,
woods!
   trees fallen, tilted, upright,
  tangles of vine and brush
  spawn pools, fungus erupting from trunks
wood you can crumble, leaf-pulp

a muskrat
   skips into the creek, dives out of sight
    a turtle dozes coldly on a snag

this is her realm
moss
slabs of trickling stone and tiny ferns
deep caves
shadow people slipping out of sight.

At the caves at Font-de-Gaume
where the deer and bison float
on bulges in the rockface

I felt the way
I feel in a cathedral.

No, better:
closer to home.

9.

Nearly the middle of March, snow everywhere
and I'm watching three winter finches,
"sparrows dipped in raspberry juice,"
take turns at the neighbor's feeder.

Winter won't let go.
Under our pine a half-starved possum
chews sunflower seeds
watched by disgusted squirrels.

My body sees all this
but my spirit is somewhere else
crossing a potato field in Poland
merged with some poor fugitive
pursued by the SS
forty-two years ago.

Later, I know, they will torture us.

Crouched in a hazel copse,
freckled with light and panting.

What causes we have to be speechless—
this century, shuddering toward its close,
has worked and twisted us
until there seems to be nothing
but muteness or scream . . .

10.

I shake my liar's head.

I've never been in Poland.

What is the etymology of "torment"?

Why has the possum been willing
to come so close to the house?

I know I imagined that albatross . . .

What will the SS men
do with my mud-caked shoes?

"Listen," I try to tell them,
"fill these with good black dirt
and plant a seed in each."

Plough us all in and try again.

Rolling toward spring, this earth,
this March of nineteen eighty-four.

January–March 1984

1.

In an old scrub orchard
a mile or two from Everyville
I see a naked couple
maybe it's you and me
around the end of August
doing something by moonlight
that could involve a search
for love or buried treasure
or something good to eat
it's just too dim from here
to tell exactly what
but I know our movements make
a lot of sense to us . . .

A line and a turn and a new line
and something fresh each time
and the lie spins round on its toe
and is, by God, the truth.

2.

The reservoir once more, on a still evening,
great gold and purple doings in the west.
Things are so still just now that it takes minutes
to pick out any motion: a ripple spreading slowly
from where a bluegill rose, a faint stir in the milkweeds,
nothing much livelier than a rusting Plymouth . . .

Motion's a lie? Rest is a bigger one.
I can take movement and all that it implies,
the skid and stub of fact, fits, fists and shakes,
heart-murmurs, toe and heel, love and its bristling opposites,

muskrat ramble and turkey strut, these gnats
making formations so complicated
they might not be patterns at all. I think
I'll move my bones around this shore
while there's still light to see.

3.
October three. Jade-green, Plum Creek slides by,
pocked with small rings and bubbles
                    twin-rimmed circles
that spread and overlap and coast the current.

        And the face in the tree is howling.

        I pace across the grass. Curled copper leaves
are half-entreating hands with cupped
                    reflections of the day.
The dice jump in the box. Rain falls.

        And the face in the tree is howling.

        Glass beads line the undersides of twigs. A sparrow
dives in a juniper bush, then fires
                    out the other side, intent upon
a pattern of his own in this good rain—

        And the face in the tree is howling.

4.
"Rabbits in Alabama hop," I wrote in 1963,
happy enough between two deaths: a summer friend
and a November president. New-married, love-sheathed,
I could feel the planet's wobble and bounce
as I walked my dog through weeds and stubble

grasshoppers spraying in every direction
so that I called myself "hub of a wheel,"
teasing my sturdy little ego
tingling along like a streetcar,
not yet in the undertow of fatherhood,
soft shoe in the cornfield, dust-mote dance,
loving the action I saw spread out—
a map of this generous, jumping-bean country.

5.

Industrial sky this afternoon, gray rags
swabbing a dim chrome button.
I seem to hear a drum and tambourine.

The branches are wiggling in thundery wind
and the last few leaves, washed from the trees,
sail through my line of sight.

Everything's moving. We never know that.
Molecules vibrate in the solid rock
out of our ken, an act of faith.

Even if helium freezes, Margaret tells me,
it's two degrees above absolute zero
and there's movement, however sluggish.

In the Milky Way's heart a magnet pulses.
Holy Ghost, spraying neutrinos and gamma rays,
come closer to our stethoscope!

•

Edmund Spenser has a headache
from trying to write *The Faerie Queene:*
Has come to court a little tipsy.

Watching the regal bitch
whirl through a wild lavolta,
her face a grinning, red-wigged skull,

"I hear the music of the spheres,"
he mutters to himself,
"and it's the dance of death."

But life and death are tango partners, Ned,
mincing through figures, cheek to cheek,
we cannot hope to read.

                    More leaves spin by,
minnows off the willows, oak-brown batwings.
And the trees rock in the giant pulse. And hold.

                    7.
A London Saturday. One year ago.
C. and I walk through the V and A,
happy to study replicas. Half a mile off
the Irish Republican Army
has car-bombed a street next to Harrods.
Blood
and broken glass
and a strange hush. Elsewhere,
a waiter drizzles oil on a salad.
In our flat near Baker Street
my wife reads, turning pages.
Bright fibers rim a shawl. Pink candles
infuse a churchy gloom.
Smell of ammonia from somewhere.
A guard yawns. A madman squints.
Hung by its feet,
a pheasant sways in a butcher's window.
Leaves blow in the park.

Time bleeds.
Holly bushes glitter.

Once again I do not know
how this can be turned into words
and held steady
even for a moment:
it slides across your eye
and flickers in your mind.

You look up from the page.

9.

I'm watching the brown tangle of tomato vines
in our December garden. They don't move.

If everything is dancing
even beyond our senses
and even if it's mad and random,
that must help explain consciousness,
perched in the body, bird in a tree,
chirps, preens, looks wildly about,
even when dozing is alert,
metabolism racing,
beady-eye, singsong, flutter and shit—

If consciousness could match the body better
and be a bear
and even hibernate?

Oh then it would miss fine things!

On Christmas Eve it snowed
as if we lived in a greeting card.
The snow blowing off the roof

and through the back-yard floodlight
as we watched from around the fire
made intricate patterns: scallops, loops,
tangles and alphabets. We're seeing the wind,
we realized, dressed
in powdery snow. Nothing to worship,
but something to wonder at,
a little epiphany, in season.

Pigeons in Buffalo, Holub told me,
can hear the Concorde landing in New York.
So what do we think we know? All of our dancing
is done in the dark, on the ceiling, the page, over the gorge
on the bridge of rotten rope and sturdy instinct.

I think I did worship that wind.

Belief is a move from branch to branch.
It doesn't much matter where you perch.
You may be hearing the Concorde. You may not.

                    10.
And yesterday a red-tailed hawk
killed and ate a mourning dove
in the middle of a snowstorm
in our back yard. For five minutes
that made a violent, bobbing center
for everything else in sight:
the swirl of flakes, the pine boughs humped with snow,
the smaller birds who fled,
our curious eyes and breath.
And then the center shifted.

Any still point we choose
is relative to observation;

the planet rolled ahead, dragging
its dead and gorgeous moon,
great storms shot up on the sun,
whole galaxies stood by and gleamed,
and maybe an owl in a hollow tree
two hundred yards away from us
swiveled his head and blinked,
hearing the little death.
The hawk rose up, his tail a flare of rust,
and a sprinkle of torn feathers
began to blow across the blood-patched snow
till we could see no more.

September 1984–February 1985

III. THE LIGHT SHOW

1.

Light breaks, the Welshman said,
where no sun shines. And Uncle Ezra spoke
of light that was not of the sun.
On Metaphor Hill I met my match.

A butterfly hovers at the windowpane.
She's gone. That was my sunshine.
Or thereabouts. I find no light
except what was, an afterglow of love,

and then this stuff that wags and pants
across the day. Good light. Good dog.
Ten lines to sunset. Later on
by starlight I may meet her?

Don't I wish. "His wife's dead,"
they say. "He must be stunned." Indeed.
Light breaks. I break. Good egg.
Good Doctor Astrov meets his match.

2.

Today the April light is fizzing.
The wind is blowing chunks of it around:
it oils pine needles, runs up tree trunks,
and spreads in clumps across the grass.
The grackles struggle darkly to resist it,
but it glosses their necks with purple and green
and slicks their beaks. I too
feel misery start to slip away—against my grain
I'm hoisted up into this giant light-machine
and swept away. My silver pen

skates on the yellow paper, my fingernails glow,
my eyes glisten with tears and pleasure.
A huge willow has fallen in my yard,
victim of wind. But today the other trees
are holding themselves up like song into a sky
that's blue with a radiance no one could imagine.

3.

Gaze of Apollo that kindled Rilke
even in a headless torso.
                          Maybe *because*
it was piecemeal.
                          We need shadows,
smoked glass, spiritual parasols. Caravaggio
knew how contingent light is, how
it comes from the wrong side, lighting
lovers and murderers indifferently.
                          Well, we *are*
star-ash. Residue. Cooling sizzle
from an old mayhem of the sun.

Galactic epigones and afterlights.

And we love light *and* shade,
color and just a little dazzle.
If I called you a feather on the breath of God,
you'd want to know what color? Right!
Different if it were white, in thin noon breeze,
or black, zigzagging through dusk's pines,
or brown, at dawn, upon an olive river . . .

4.

Rodin, I learn,
liked his wax version of *The Gates of Hell*

for its "blond shadows." Who doesn't love
light's pleasing accidents and glances?
The casual star my dropped keys make,
the wren's flight, a molecule of deity
cut loose, both particle and wave,
chaos across the retina, then night,
scaring the daylights out of the west.

And Proust remembered a restaurant front
"glazed and streaming with light."
I think of your lit skin, your limbs and breasts
when we made love by firelight. It may be
that all my poems celebrating light
have had your beauty as their subtext.
But I'll not hand the grief-cup round . . .

Edward Lear, the epileptic,
disappointed painter, found
the English daylight fickle:
"a tree is black one minute,
the next it's yellow, and the 3rd green;
so that were I to finish any part
the whole would be all spots—
a sort of Leopard Landscape."
He wrestled his easel back to the studio.

Light the Leopard. Springs in the new year.
Us he devours? But the wren lives on.
Lear is remembered for his limericks,
his ready nonsense. Spotted and inconstant,
we love the life we say we yearn to lose.

7.
At our Midsummer Party
we tried to have all kinds of light:

a bonfire, candles, Tahiti torches,
fireflies adding their dots on the dark;
we set off pinwheels, Roman candles,
brandished sparklers—and later, above embers,
we were content with starlight.
I was a little miserable. I thought
myself on the other shore of love;
the pinwheels were for the sun's renewal,
not for mine. My mind went back
to the sun's other birthday,
that Christmas Eve we read "The Dead"
and watched the snow in the floodlight.

Love makes the world precious? Yes,
and loss of ego brings on love,
snow sifting off the roof
to blow where the night wind takes it . . .

8.

Georgia,
even your snapshot
fills me with singing light.
You're holding Tom, you're standing next to
an amiable priest who came to bless the fields.
You're looking out at the world with love and trust,
giving yourself, steady as a lamp.
The tears that filled me up
fill with light now:
mountain light, sea light,
midsummer light, Christmas light.
Refraction. Rilke spoke his hope:
"That this homely weeping might bloom."
And Tu Fu imagined the moonlight
drying the tear-tracks on two faces.
Whatever happens to me in this life,

including the blow that finally knocks me dead,
your light will remind me to love and praise,
the day coming up again,
the world enacting its own beginnings,
and everything moving in this earthshine.

9.

Earthrise: from its rubbled moon
I'm watching the sun's third planet.

It's blue and white, with flecks of brown and green.
Vast weather systems swirl and mottle it.
Moist, breathing through its fantastic
membrane of atmosphere,
it crowds my heart with love.

The world's suspended, Chekhov says,
on the tooth of a dragon. Even that tooth gleams.

I've come here to figure out how light
streams to the wheeling planet,
a solar blast, photons and protons,
and helps it live. Morowitz
and Lewis Thomas tell us
that energy from the sun
doesn't just flow to earth
and radiate away: "It is
thermodynamically inevitable
that it must rearrange
matter into symmetry,
away from probability,
against entropy,
lifting it, so to speak,
into a constantly changing

condition of rearrangement
and molecular ornamentation."

Which is how I got here, I suppose,
some rearranged matter
imagining and praising
"a chancy kind of order,"
always about to be chaos again,
"held taut
against probability
by the unremitting
surge of energy"
streaming out of the sun.

Behind, above, below me, stars:
countless suns with the same meaning!

Before me, leisurely as a peacock,
the turning earth.

10.
It's a late October afternoon:
warm winds and distant thunder.
Leaves catch the sunlight as they shower down.

Just over my outstretched fingertips
floats Emily Dickinson, horizontal spirit:
"See all the light, but see it slant,"
is what she seems to murmur.

I don't know. All through these months
I've been a well with two buckets:
one for grief and one for love.
Sometimes the daylight has bewildered me.

A day as bright and intricate as a crystal,
an afternoon that will not go away—
one of time's strange suspensions.

The Gospel Lighthouse Church's lemon-yellow bus
says "Heaven Bound" up front. They feel they know.
Last night, what made me think
we are continuous with a noumenal world
was a sheet of blank paper in my midnight bedroom
rising and falling in a midnight breeze.

This afternoon my house
is flooded with late sunlight
and the next sheet of paper after this one
is blank and is for you.

March–October 1985

The Portable Earth-Lamp

The planet on the desk, illuminated globe
we ordered for Bo's birthday,
sits in its Lucite crescent, a medicine ball
of Rand McNally plastic. A brown cord
runs from the South Pole toward a socket.

It's mostly a night-light for the boys,
and it blanches their dreaming faces,
a blue sphere patched with continents,
mottled by deeps and patterned currents,
its capital cities bright white dots.

Our models: they're touching and absurd,
magical both for their truth and falsehood.

I like its shine at night. Moth-light.
I sleepwalk toward it, musing.
This globe's a bible, a bubble of myth-
light, a blue eye, a double
bowl: empty of all but its bulb and clever skin,
full of whatever we choose to lodge there.

I haven't been able to shake off all my grief,
my globe's cold poles and arid wastes,
the weight of death, disease and history.
But see how the oceans heave and shine,
see how the clouds and mountains glisten!

We float through space. Days pass.
Sometimes we know we are part of a crystal

where light is sorted and stored,
sharing an iridescence
cobbled and million-featured.

Oh tiny beacon in the hurting dark.
Oh soft blue glow.

from

The Planet on the Desk

Visionary's Ghazal

Acorn clicking like a lunatic crystal,
A bud in loam, a time bomb full of forests.

Tiger-striped, the sun through winter trees.
Zebra-barred, the moon in the naked windbreak.

Thunder punching through branches & flimsy windows,
Lightning mating with a hapless maple.

The hills slope to the river like fast music.
Banjos scuttle like centipedes, fiddles wheel like bats.

Sucking the huge stone breast, tonguing its rusty tit,
In a spray of dandruff & fingernails, a loping pulse.

Awake in a suit of hate, asleep in a gown of love.
Dancing floors of enameled sexual memory.

Scorch me, stun me, leave me alone, Reverberator;
Leave me to blood & starlight, the ringing & stilling anvil.

Root Vegetable Ghazal

The moon swings off in a bag like a market lettuce
And everyone gropes home by ant glint & beetle shine.

In the Hotel Potato, in waxy marble ballrooms,
The waltzers rustle to the croon of enzymes.

In the curved corridors of the onion palace,
The smell of mushrooms seeps from unlit closets.

Our city is littered with wormseed & forcemeat;
Mummies are hymning in our turnip-purple church.

Radishes cruise through the revenant storage warehouse.
The bones of a goose mark the way to an amphitheater.

Now we can scale the carrot, our tapering campanile,
To watch the platoons of gravel, the water-bead parade.

We with our thorn-wrapped hearts & ivory foreheads!
We with our mineral tunnels awash in mole-glow!

Easter Ghazal

Dreaming the dead back to life: pleasure & gentleness.
Grateful for this miracle, this bubble of reunion.

Harps bounce & hum there in the firmament.
The fundament. Coining likenesses. Did you say something?

Bricks crumb, bones powder: this helps make potting soil.
Clay reproduces! Ploughs heal the fields they wound.

Today we trim the rabbit's nails upside the hutch,
Nail up the bat-house, baptize each other with the hose.

I'm flame. A flag going up a flagpole. I'm
The beetle dropped by the mother bird, picked up again.

The heart's a tomato with lips. Woodpeckers tap hosannas.
Sleepy blips & explosions fleck love's radar screen.

Something rises. Something drops. Elastic days!
Tonight this window's black with possibility.

Bird Ghazal

The blue jay stabs at cracked corn. Sparrows follow.
Idiom of the beak, twelve nervous harpsichords.

The splash of blood on the woodpecker's head;
Nocturnal goatsuckers, calling you over & over.

Shooting baskets in the driveway, hitting shot after shot.
Sawing the tree down, branch by branch, while juncos watch.

The horned owl's cat face rising from its nest mess.
Big raptor seen through pines, sharp-shinned or rough-legged hawk.

Cloud causeways rimmed with ice-burn. Meager daylight.
A duck lands, skidding, on the pond's buffed surface.

These fearless black birds haunt the hotel pools.
They sail through our hegemony, omens & denials.

Otherness, otherness. Why do we stare so fondly?
A plume of seagulls trails a garbage barge.

Hamlet Ghazal

Night in the courtyard. When did your mother
First betray your father? Who cares? Who doesn't?

You see that cloud? The bird of dawning . . . sings all night.
"We could do *Tamburlaine* too, if you'd prefer that."

I will walk heere in the Hall. *Pause.* I'll do it lots.
After all, it *is* the breathing time of day for me.

These swords are of a length? These bones? Books? Plays?
And did she let you come into her closet? Did they watch?

Oh, all these questions! Let's just have some fun!
If the ghost comes back, we'll toss some nicknames at it.

And lists of lawless resolutes, long as your arm.
The squeak & gibber of that lady floating past . . .

The road to the castle. The players with their cart.
The oldest jumps into an open grave, for sport.

Worship Ghazal

Ignorance banging its head next to a beautiful doorway.
Hunger that sits down to dine on pebbles & bricks.

Tears that lie deep in the onion, hand that caresses the moon.
God has no body so we kindly lend him ours.

Night-grind that blinds us & bruises our spirit & flesh
Until we walk out & the galaxies flower around us.

"Emptiness takes us into its craving," the poet says.
Now I am breathing evenly, watching the stir of the wind.

The crude yellow stars that bloom on the pumpkin vine:
Even these features can riddle the senses with glee.

The raspberries drag their canes back down to the grass.
Horse mushrooms rise up like dinner plates waiting for apples.

The rainbow begins on the earth & returns to it.
The carnival torch you held & forgot burns forever.

from

Night Thoughts and Henry Vaughan

Henry Vaughan

1. MOUNTAIN HARE

I rise as the moon sets
and dawn beats up confusion.
Out on the mountain, walking,
I round a hedge in changing light
and meet a full-grown hare.

For a moment we stand and stare
fixed by the shock of each other.

He's big as a goat. His ears twitch,
dew shines on his coat,
his wild walleye glitters
and then I fall inside it
and wake an hour or a minute later.

Poor Doctor Vaughan's gone off again.
Maybe that's what they say in the town.

2. GLOWWORMS AND STRAWBERRIES

Follows me everywhere, this light,
and speaks to me in tongues.

It's the light that strawberries give off
whether or not you cut them in half.

It's the mute and muted light
earthworms admire in glowworms.

It's a candle inside a bottle
inside another bottle,

the third-hand light of the pond-moon
that dazzles us down to the backbone.

Light buds and sprouts like plants.
The body fills and shivers.

The spray on the blossoming trees
makes a solid wall of surf

across the hillside orchard
as the world spins slowly, wobbling.

Honeybees weave and dart
bright on their patterned errands.

Light slides through the broad river,
rising like trout in the pools,

and finds itself in the music
that running water makes all night.

No matter how bad we've made the world,
killing for Charles or Cromwell,

it's God, it's made of God,
and will survive.

3. NIGHT-PIECE

I have walked past mountain outcrops
as daylight suddenly caught them,
showing the fire-glint inside.

Or sidewise, from a blacksmith's forge,
in a dusk amid horses and men,
comes a shower of sparks that fires my eye.

Maybe the night is best.
A deep, but dazzling darkness.

God coasts like a perfect boat
through coves and shoals of blackshine.

If you walk abroad you shiver
at the fat choir of stars,
and stare at the will-o'-the-wisps
dancing on swamps and meadows.

Dig your fingers into the turf
and hold for dear life to the planet.

I've called the night God's knocking-time.
I've heard his still, soft call
as he hunts like a sharp-eyed owl.

And I swear I heard him whisper
"One of your poems made me weep,"
but he never said which one.

4. HAVING LIVED THROUGH A WAR, I CAN HYMN

Dumb and warm, the sheep stroll up
to nose me on the hillside
as I lie and stare at stars.

Milk runs cold in the sky,
water walks down the valley.
I hear the bark of a fox.

Odor of smoke and magnetic sex,
weird conversation of goats.
While the Bible shines, a lamp in a box,

the galaxy strokes its beard
and fondles its giant breasts,
pregnant and sure of its death.

All Wales is dreaming through me,
all England talks in its sleep.
It is thin silk, this ecstasy,

that rips itself into music
and drinks the tears that run
across its own wet face.

5.   THE WEATHER COCK

Now here is a great joke:

the idea that the earth is finite
and we are mortal clay.

The Royal Society's saying
this world is merely "matter."
Even the clay knows better than that.

This is a world where soul-shine
blows through the clouds and trees,
where spirit bubbles in springs
and beats in lonely wells.

God's bliss sings in the weeds
and shines in the path of slugs,
the tracks that lead nowhere,

straight as the spiral that runs
like a whelk shell or the wind
spinning the weathercock over my house,
light seeding itself each night
to spiral and sprout each day.

Come to my grave in Wales.
You'll see a glistening yew
and, on an old stone wall,
you'll find a snail with a perfect shell.

You may learn that God's the light,
wind is the Holy Ghost,
and Christ's the water cycle.

Mornings, there's dew
up there on the weathercock.

The tin bird spins
and is lit by the sun.

from Night Thoughts

MIDNIGHT . . .

Deep in a blue Ohio night
a man takes out a box
of Ohio Blue Tip matches.

He's a gardener, an insomniac, a maniac,
he's me.

He strikes one, tosses it, and as he does
a meteor flares in silence overhead.

The games we play
to say we own and know the stars . . .

I crunch through a mint patch in my garden.
Above me, the Perseids streak the sky
every other minute, pen-strokes of light.

I'm going to put you in this matchbox now
and take you for a stroll around my yard.

August midnight, Ohio blue-tip night,
star-time and meteor-time,
I love the way the town goes lax,
gives itself back to the wilderness.

The daytime self gets lost, grows hair,
and marks the owl's cool questions.

Scratch of a match, wink of a star,
meteor-flare, lightning bug,
and here we go.

·

Growing older, you listen more
to memory's concertina,
squeezing time in and pulling it out.

I look at our darkened house,
everyone sleeping, unless my son
is still stretched out and reading . . .

I scratch a burnt match backward, flame
gathers itself to a blue-tipped matchhead,
and time folds back, collapses.

I walked yesterday in the graveyard
where Chloe's ashes are buried.
I had it, I think, to myself.

A hot wind rushed and shoveled its way
through the giant oaks. Dragonflies
circled the small scummed pond.

Late summer's an in-between time.
Love for the dead and the living
began to expand and bewilder me.

Strike a match here and a firefly answers,
cool gleams rise and fall
in my friendly, unfriendly yard.

The Chinese like to say
fireflies haunt fresh graves,
small tears that blink and wheel.

·

A plane winks by above me,
thoughts bunch and float, the local owl
hoots twice, a memory signals,
raspberries ripen,
and dew begins to coat my sneakers—
night's a good time for seeing.

Water-gleam, Plum Creek, frog—another pair
of upturned eyes. Sight bubbles,
bulges and bumps,
momentary domes afloat on rain-pocked streams,
those iridescent clusters at the tide line
that slide and skate as wind and wave decide,

fragility's stubborn clutch
of gene pools, breeding cells,
egg and seed cascades,
gnats that hatch and die within a day,
and hearsay: word-throngs
rushing here and there by starlight.

•

I sidle and slide toward our new screened porch
to murmur a night-hymn to Georgia:

You and I
know love can be
so open, so complete
it's breathing a different air,
it's coming out
into a light-struck world.

And we know
how fragile this mixture is,
scratch of a match,

flaring and winking out,
night-blooms in a frost-invaded garden.

There goes another meteor . . .
A whiz without the bang.

Imagination's stubborn,
Eros is kind of tongue-tied,
Nature turns her back, its back.
I'm left with meteor streaks,
thinking how Shakespeare got much closer:

Ruin hath taught me thus to ruminate
That Time will come and take my love away.

Now the new moon's setting,
through trees that keep their counsel.

A Japanese-beetle trap, bright yellow,
sways on the branch of a juniper bush
we cut down more than two years ago,
a bush that can't be there,
and the night's black glass surrounds me.

•

This carbon dark,
this diamondback night—
How many times in my life
have I walked out to see the Perseids?

How could I even count
heading toward fifty-five
here in the century's one
reversible year?

Smeared with a little Off, I move and sniff,
craning my neck like the woodchuck
who shuffles up to our deck sometimes
and peers in, myopic, to where I'm working.

·

Here's our back-lot woodpile.
I can settle myself against it, smell the pines,
and gaze across the lampblack creek
at the dim tangle of brush
and soaring trees.

All of Ohio was like this once.
I've heard a squirrel could start
from a tree by Lake Erie and travel
south to the river at Kentucky
without once touching the ground.

Why can't a mind do the same,
following impulse where it leads,
splashing across the creek just here,
climbing the bitter sycamore,
soaring out toward these constellations?

All of us are sad Prince Hamlet *and*
the gravedigger he jokes with,
juggling old skulls
out in the boneyard
under the starlight.

·

Hearing my muttering,
the woodchuck raises up to watch me.

So many dead
the old earth harbors by now—
war dead, plague dead, infants, mothers,
sprawled, hunched, staring, rigid,
Indians, settlers, branching forebears
twisted up in roots—
the planet's one vast graveyard.

Now the hair
stands up
on the back
of my neck.

Spirits are fuming and circling all around me.
Half here, half somewhere else,
lives inside out, they hiss and sigh.

This may be Pound I'm fighting off.
Lie quiet, Ezra. And this one
may be Whitman. Of course I love you, Walt.

And now it's over, they're melting back
into bushes, trees, and grass. Once more,
the night's my empty mirror.

Wait.
One figure's left,
a big man, treading slowly like a cat
across damp grass.

Ghost from Hartford, ghost from Reading,
here for an ordinary evening . . .

•

I venture a sort of salute. He shows
his teeth.

For something to be nonsense,
you have to know what sense is, right?
All you postmodernists are such pachyderms,
what should I say to you about my poems?

I danced with all the scientists
and hardly anyone knew it. Chaos and nonsense are
the little bit of leaven in the bread,
the little bit of heaven in the head . . .

A star streaks north in a long arc.
He shakes his silver head.

Time to be off now, boy, he mutters.
Remember me! The leaves flicker and shiver.
A barred owl hoots. He's gone.

ONE A.M. . . .

What was that phantom up to?

Close-up of my ear: it drank his blue words in
and stored them up. He said
he knew some things
we think we've just discovered:
sense and nonsense
depend upon each other—
order and chaos.

•

Above me,
half-visible, the trees
stir in the wind, green calmness

stalking across the summer, breathing oxygen
to make us tingle and rise
like mushrooms from across the cosmos.

Beyond, the occasional meteors
on night's starred face.

Up on the dark screened porch
the book on physics I've been reading
murmurs of comets and of Nemesis:

Imagine a star, twin to our sun,
that moves in a huge, looped orbit
and sets off comet showers
whenever it swings too close.

Could it be
that comet showers

drove our fitful evolution,
made us the clever, puzzled things we are,
thriving on catastrophes,
ice ages?

Even my own back yard
is a doorway, a black hole,
where oceans and eons mingle,
on the border of sense and nonsense,
as I walk the property line, arms out.

                          •

Illumination night, that's what this is!
What kind of light do we really yearn for?
Lightning that splits the world open for a second?
Heat-lightning, maybe, that safer pulse
that stutters at the horizon? Firefly-bloom?

Today the breeze blew, the sun shone hot,
and daylight put gleams and flecks
on every leaf, like Constable, tongue
between his teeth, lighting his painting up
with a white-tipped brush.

But this darkness suits a poet best,
spirit-fucker, bone arranger: all
we need is a faint gleam now and then,
some moonlight staggering in foliage
or a meteor sliding down night's black throat.

In this bad light
where sounds are muffled too
I can slip out of my gnostic pelt
and whoever I summon may come:
Constable, Dyson, Stevens, Edward Young.

•

But the dark isn't light enough now.
The night's too quiet,
shadows are much too deep.
I'm starting to sweat a cold sweat.

I runne to death, and death meets me as fast,
And all my pleasures are like yesterday.

Who turned the tables on me here?
What swan rides through what gates?
I fumble for my little verbal amulet.

Straighten up, remember who you are.
You spoke of beetle shine and ant glint.
You went to earth, the grave smelled good to you.
You hymned the light, the waves and particles,
you made the words come shyly to their clearings.

You'll show that toad-eater who wrote *Night Thoughts*
what's happened in two centuries or so.

You'll make your yard the spirit's doorway
to metamorphs and comet-lit inventions.

Go ahead, walk the cathedral-volumned night.
Let Perseids stripe your eyes.

•

I read the other day
that giant black snowballs from outer space
created our oceans.

Center me, physics, keep me
from brooding too long on my fear,
on the pickup truck that rammed the school bus,
on the strange sea pastures of the Persian Gulf,
on love and its string of losses.

Now everything's strings, they say, cosmic strings
that pull the galaxies toward the Great Attractor
holding all matter together.

Microcosm, meet macrocosm.
Solace us with your kinship, make
one little yard an everywhere.

I think of Calvino's
dark, humorous mind,
another squirrel in the treetops—
how he made truth and wit
from troubling loops of knowledge.

And Miroslav Holub,
who lived in this house alone one spring
and pondered this yard as I do.
The appetite for fact
helped him survive, walk around
and laugh to himself, inside
this century's bluntest terrors—
the one that Hitler made,
the one that Stalin added.

A string may link me to them here,
and run
right through the blackened school bus,
the rubble of Beirut,
down to the toxic wastes, up and out
to the ice ball punching our stratosphere—

Like Theseus in his labyrinth,
I stand here holding
my little end of string.

●

I caught and cupped a firefly just now
like an old miser blowing on his palms
to keep some warmth in.

I'd like that glow to be
a tiny window to infinity
blazing with false cheer.

I've climbed to a branch of our sour-cherry tree
to gaze toward the darkened freighter called my house,
cruising the night seas.
Man overboard, I whisper.
A spider rides my forearm.

Ruin hath taught me thus to ruminate
That Time will come and take my love away.
  This thought is as a death, which cannot choose
  But weep to have that which it fears to lose.

●

I had this dream last night,
and maybe not just once:

At first I saw the horses from above
as they were being harnessed to the sledge.

They dropped me off a mile or so
from the deserted, snowbound farm.

Maybe I snowshoed in,
maybe I walked.

I remember the pearl silence,
the sense of peace that comes with dawn in winter.

Working steadily, I shoveled paths
to the barn, the chicken run, the corn crib,

I swept the grainy snow away
from the porch and weathered kitchen door,

let myself in with an ancient, six-inch key,
strolled the deserted rooms, fingered mementos,

stoked up the furnace and lit the stoves,
pumped water at the sink, wiped off the counter,

and then stood looking out
across the empty fields.

The clear windows of the silent farmhouse,
the wide fields and ghostly outbuildings,

an old hay wagon
coated with fresh snow:

somewhere the horses
steamed and stamped,

waiting to take me,
but I prolonged my dream.

Hands in my pockets I gazed
as if I could never see enough.

·

Repetition's magic. I knew it in my bones.
Let me repeat my dream for you,
let me repeat it for myself.
Let me talk on in this starlight,
these meteor streakings of nonsense,
this chaos, these fractals and freckles.

I'm losing the dream farm,
I'm probably failing, repeating
what others have said—
but that farm, like an old brown photograph
suddenly filling the senses—
and this night, like a silver gelatin print—
and a string that runs from me to the past:
the view from the farmhouse window
across the silent fields of snow.

This Swiss-cheese reality
I leave things out of—I meant to say
that the water falls up to the pump
and then freezes again, or the milk
rises in strings from the pail
to fill the great soft udder.

Did I really think I had Time
by the scruff of the neck for once?

I knock ice loose and work the pump again.
I taste that water, drink my dream,
run it like an old home movie
until it fades and turns to nonsense.

I'm spreading a quilt on the grass
the better to watch these meteors zip
the night's black motorcycle jacket.

I want a myth that will unfurl the starlight—
the story of the loss and gaze
of the first singer, Orpheus.

•

I used to tell this story to my family.
I'd miss the point deliberately and stress
the sentiment—rapt stones
and animals and trees, the iron teardrops
rolling down Pluto's cheek . . .

Did I conceal
the truer meanings from my children
or myself?

The point is Eurydice's veiled face,
death and mystery, fetched
back into daylight.

If you are Orpheus, even briefly,
you can go deep into darkness, find her,
draw her along behind you
and bring her back up to the world,

but only by keeping your back to her,
turning away—
you act unconcerned,
you ignore in order to find.

In this hovering moment of truth,
this poise, this hush—
darkness illuminates,
fullness and emptiness are twins,
and then it collapses because you forgot
the magic, the rules.
You swivel to look, the veil grows opaque,
she's gone.

You cry out—roots and dirt
sift through your fingers,
the grave-smell rises,
dark's dark, empty's empty.

There's nothing
to see or to sing about.
You've lost her
twice.

•

I look back at what I've done—it sags
and nears collapse. I look for what I sought—
it slides behind a veil. I kiss the veil,
no, there's no veil there now.
Even a word like *void* is much too rich.
Ennui's more like it, *anomie,*
words I can scarcely bring myself to say.

But wait—I think a look would change it.
A look can cut down trees, unravel knots,
make creatures tame, sing stones to sleep.

Lost twice is twice as bad,
or does the second loss
forgive the first and then itself?

The song's not yours to understand or own.
You let it go as you must let her go.
You may or may not find another song.

The night's great grindstone throws another spark.

The owl sails noiseless among midnight trees.

Here comes our cat across the grass,
her ears alert for every night-sound.

We're halfway home, I tell her,
purring. I've learned my lesson,
no doubt I'll soon forget it. Mystery
lives in the darkness and comes to my hand.

I give it up, it gives me up—
we're here together in the dark.

•

My back-yard memories branch like antlers.

Lost moments are surfacing tonight
like whales on a moonlit ocean. I recall
a canvas hammock spotted by cherry pits
dropped by the feasting birds.

There, mid-yard,
we built a snow fort once that stood
housing its own coldness for a week or two.

And down by the creek a half-built raft
waited through much of a summer to be launched.

Blue-black fruits of darkness,
memory-berries.

•

Always we thought the yard ours, flying kites,
throwing sticks for the dog, tossing baseballs,
croquet and tonic, food at the splintery table,
but when we went in, and we always did,
the animals had it back again—

they came and went, as they always do,
the possum with her dull-orange eyeshine
and prehistoric face,
echolocating bats and shifty rabbits,
the moles who tunnel through their routine night,
shrews, muskrats, skunks, even a fox and cubs.

There's a big dome-backed raccoon around here now.
He skulked past in daylight last week,
a mouse in his mouth, ringed tail, black mask,
an ambulatory teakettle!

He's one of the spirits of this place,
cutting across God's orchard,
piss-elegant raider, scrubbing his food in the creek.

Hopkins was right:
the way things manifest being
ought to send lightning bolts through us.

The cat licking her turned-up paw
or simply blinking in the morning sun
is enough to make me wide-eyed.

Lives populate this acre,
something to set against nothingness.
I freeze, delighted, whenever a snake slides past.

•

Dig down in this yard and you find clay—
its microcrystals might have taught
proteins a way to replicate.

Up from crude soup to tangled bank,
symmetry fracturing, healing, fracturing,
till we get to the robust ecology
of woodchucks, gardens, fireflies, and me.

I don't know genetic drift from Adam.
I gaze at a woodpecker or an azalea
and the whole mess makes me glad.

Then I want to tidy it.

We're more like bees
than we care to admit—

we have to have our symmetries,
our hives and honeycombs.

They rise from our dreams,
live in our brains, filling our language,

we advance into chaos
like needles and threads, like zippers,
leaving connections behind us,
creating our structures
so we can love them and destroy them,
naming the constellations
so we can learn to forget them.

Is the woodchuck asleep in his tunnels
or is he at large tonight?

A mouse listens, a wide-awake owl
lifts one foot, then another,

FOUR A.M. . . .

Night sky, spore drift, black sponge,
a countryside alive with silver bees,
smoke in a forest clearing washed by lightning:

roaming my yard,
bleary and sick at heart come 4 a.m.,
I've reached a kind of bottom.

How little I know my own world;
now, as I stroll below these meteor streaks,
I give up trying to own my yard, my life.

·

What in the world is language, sir,
and what in language is the world?

Why should I weave another word-nest,
resting spot for my fly-by-night self,
and make it ask these questions?

Rain falls to earth and then evaporates.
Language may be a wheel that never rests.

·

I should retire to some asylum
and reconstruct Omaha from toothpicks.
I'd be more honest with myself.

I tell myself, Stop fumbling around
in the past and present.

Stop stringing these necklaces
of order and belief.

Stop munching the macaroons of history.

•

Below you is no city but a night
where thousands of Ohio fireflies
flash in deep meadows and still fields.

This is a garden, whatever else it is.
This is a yard; that deep and winking view
was from the local reservoir.

A heron coasts across the starlit water,
the corn breathes quietly, the night wheels past.
Owls call from windbreaks, then are still.

You think you make the night again in words.
They just as much make you.
That's what the fireflies are signaling.

Your system is and isn't metaphor.
It lives, you live,
among the hidden structures of the night.

FIVE A.M. . . .

An hour or so before dawn
a gradual milkiness starts to tinge the air.

High up, two crows pass over,
as if they expected the sun
to rearrange our world
with energy and light.

The nullity I feel
becomes euphoria. Look,
we have survived another night.

Our lives, the brief and anxious days,
have been extended once again.

•

One last stroll around Young's acre,
stars in their parking spaces
trees in their dreamy sockets and the dead
tucked in their jars and crates.

On my old apple tree back here
are knobbly fruit you'd hardly want to pick;
but the taste behind the uninviting skin
is a perfect burst of sweet and tart.

Take one, bite once, let the taste explode,
your thirst turns into joy and you
can toss the sampled lump across the creek.
Now take another. Savor the stored-up weather.

Here are the giant rusting glasses
a student sculptor won a prize with,

then had to leave behind,
six hundred pounds of steel.

I perch on them to note
they frame the eyes of nothing
which then look out
at nothing.

Here's our compost bin, warm and a little stinky,
cuttings and garbage turning back into humus.
A sort of immortality—
if you're not particular about your ego.

"The universe is still dead," says Polanyi,
"but it already has the capacity
of coming to life." It's a self-excited circuit.
And so am I, and so's this self-adjusting poem.

•

The woodchuck's gone, the owl's asleep,
the toads and turtles hop and creep away.
The meteors join the sunlight.

What the trees sang, what the stars whistled,
what science hummed and danced—
a truth or two about my house and yard.

A night made out of meteors and fireflies,
a poem set to come to terms with Time.
A ramble of a thousand lines or so.

•

Now I am very still, tailor-fashion on the bricks
of our small terrace.

Look, I am seeing nothing.

The pre-dawn cool has lulled the world asleep.
Mosquitoes and fireflies are gone.

My mouth is set, my eyes are shut.

Systems and patterns and synapse-leaps
are shutting down inside me.

A flag of pure light starts to unfurl now

beyond the eastern trees. Birdsong starting up.
The star-shower night is over. Time

warps itself straight and pulls away

toward the horizon. The muddy obligations
reassert themselves. A secret country

closes its tingling books. This nocturne

spools back into the ebony piano.
I am still far from that condition

where suffering can't be told from joy,

but I have sensed it once again.
Great kiss of sunrise and a little breeze

and the light comes through the trees like wine

like conflagration,
like a blazing angel.

•

The sun comes up and takes me one day closer.
And I open my clenched fists,
as I promised I would for this portrait.

I do it finger by finger; right hand first,
with its crooked index and stubby thumb,
my small lifelong deformity.

The blank palm, like an absent face,
makes you ask what's hidden in the left.
I open that now too.

One finger wears an old gold ring.
You can see this hand's more dexterous,
that it has a more interesting palm.

But it's empty too, as I foretold you.
I'm the sleight-of-hand man still
here in this summer sunrise.

I told you I'd have nothing.
Palms open,
hands extended.

Wait. Now look again.

from

At the White Window

Poem for Adlai Stevenson and Yellow Jackets

It's summer, 1956, in Maine, a camp resort
on Belgrade Lakes, and I am cleaning fish,
part of my job, along with luggage, firewood,
Sunday ice cream, waking everyone
by jogging around the island every morning
swinging a rattle I hold in front of me
to break the nightly spider threads.
Adlai Stevenson is being nominated,
but won't, again, beat Eisenhower,
sad fact I'm half-aware of, steeped as I am
in Russian novels, bathing in the tea-
brown lake, startling a deer and chasing it by canoe
as it swims from the island to the mainland.
I'm good at cleaning fish: lake trout,
those beautiful deep swimmers, brown trout,
I can fillet them and take them to the cook
and the grateful fisherman may send a piece
back from his table to mine, a salute.
I clean in a swarm of yellow jackets,
sure they won't sting me, so they don't,
though they can't resist the fish, the slime,
the guts that drop into the bucket, they're mad
for meat, fresh death, they swarm around
whenever I work at this outdoor sink
with somebody's loving catch.
Later this summer we'll find their nest
and burn it one night with a blowtorch
applied to the entrance, the paper hotel
glowing with fire and smoke like a lantern,
full of the death-bees, hornets, whatever they are,
that drop like little coals

and an oily smoke that rolls through the trees
into the night of the last American summer
next to this one, thirty-six years away, to show me
time is a pomegranate, many-chambered,
nothing like what I thought.

Wind, Rain, Light

The drooling roof of an old barn overhead,
the sup and chuckle of water.
                              Nineteen sixty-four
and it's spring, or the first cold edge of it.
        We've started a child, Chloe and I,
my seed taking hold in her
                              as roots wake
birds stir and puzzle out their nests,
nights shining weirdly,
                              days wind-scoured.
        Clear water rills and wrinkles in the gutters,
snowmelt, purposeful as bees.
        The sunlight
blisters it, dazzles it,
                              plays its own music
on the water's harp, and the sky stands still
to let the new clouds pass,
                              white-knuckled.
        I have my car, a Studebaker,
glinting, already obsolete, I race
straight down old Highway 20,
                              yelling *Avanti!*,
light-drunk, wind-riddled, energy
rolling in waves
                    across the furrowed fields
while the black storms of our separate deaths
are forming: hers, now passed,
mine on the flat horizon,
very far off, even his, the child's,
as the fetus blooms,
                    as life takes shape,
blackness too soft to understand,
blackness we go back to,

breathing deep, still deeper,

                                cupfuls of air,
our lungs like double buckets in a well,
filling ourselves with air-shine, a faint mist
hovering all around us,

                                drizzle, filament, bead,
wipers ticking and streams of April rain
crossing the hood and roof,
spinning off,

                        another line of storms approaching,
sheets and curtains, miles of rain
crossing the plains,

                          wavering rise and fall,
crackle of lightning,

                              thundery dust and leaves
whirl up to meet the downpour.

        Lake Erie churning and all of Ohio
flattened by rain,

                    my car nosing like a boat
through spumes and side-blasts.

        This
life!

        I put my hand out,

                    reaching toward
my own face mirrored in the car,
tears that stream and mingle with the rain,
great hive of separate drops,

                            temple of spray and light,
no longer needing to know

                      what anything means.

Lessons in Metaphysics

The stepladder lies on its side,
    meaning nothing at all.

I put on a compact disc—
    a pianist comes into the room,

although, of course, he's not here.
    Soon he is joined by an orchestra.

Outside, disorderly honeysuckles
    open their blossoms, one by one,

the sway and drag of June—
    each rhododendron, each azalea.

You still don't get it?
    Wait for the next boat,

wait for the swan,
    the crow, even the sparrow.

Perhaps, though, you'll never get it
    until there's no you and no it . . .

My Mother at Eighty-Eight

Shrunken like an old sweet apple
out of a half-forgotten orchard,
her mind as hollow as an apple seed,
she greets me now, her middle child,
without the least idea of who I am.

Her eyes glitter. Nothing behind them.

Or has she journeyed to a prairie
where all our codes and grids have been abandoned,
no houses, no towns, no roads—clear sky,
a few clouds riding aimlessly across it,
and a bird or two, meadowlarks probably,
tossing around in its depths?

Landscape with Grief Train

Such a huge locomotive, the grief train,
panting, ugly, shiny, and black,
but it has many cars to pull
and a very long distance to travel.

Miraculously, it needs no fuel,
having the one event, or many,
to keep it going for eternity
—or however long you imagine.

Sometimes you see it at crossings.
You're headed somewhere else.
Perhaps you've been laughing a lot,
or just come from seeing a movie.

The great thing about it, of course,
is its steadiness and drive. You forget it,
and still it is going to be out there,
snaking through mountain passes,

rushing all night next to white-flecked rivers,
hooting its soundless whistle,
and sending on up toward the stars
its smoke, which is pungent and cold.

My Father at Ninety-Four

When you have gone away for good
I think I'll hang a mirror by the door
hoping that you can visit, quiet man,
sometimes as a bird, or a dawn,
or a cloud around the moon.

When the mirror is open and empty
and I happen to pass it myself,
say, in a fine October twilight,
you will be there too, sometimes,
behind my eyes, calm and resigned.

When I can no longer find you, hear you,
I will go see the Great Plains again
and walk around the places
you took me to, a dance
of trees, farms, people, sky.

Stone City, Strawberry Point,
Spearfish Canyon, Estes Park,
Lake of the Isles, Yellowstone,
Nebraska sand hills, Wyoming sky,
towns almost as lost as Mesa Verde.

A son and a father, still shy about touch,
I'll pretend I can put my hand in yours
from a greater distance, like two men
who stand on separate hills and wave
as daylight goes on to its rest.

Landscape with Wolves

Council Bluffs, Iowa. 1750s & 1950s

All that summer they could hear the wolves
as the tribes gathered on the Iowa side,
wolves out under the stars, in the distance
that jumps away when you stand on the cliffs
facing the river and hills to the west.

And then it was later, two hundred years,
and there was a city among the hills,
ambulance sirens, Omaha's lights
thicker than stars, and the same great river
winding its course to the southeast.

I would go up there on summer nights
and I swear to you the wolves would come out:
bodies of wolves, the tips of their voices
calling the stars and the tribes together,
just as if time was a totally different story.

Landscape with Bees

Santa Giuliana, Umbria. 1995

Another morning on this mountain,
    goat bells, butter-colored broom,
a few clouds bunching in the south,
    milk-foam, silk mattress stuffing.

Someone is swimming in the horse pond,
    someone's exploring the hillside.
Like me, the lizards on the rocky wall
    are poleaxed by the sunshine.

To be able to read a page—say Virgil's *Georgics*—
    and then glance up
across a gulf of laundered air
    at a brother mountain, fifteen miles away . . .

•

Old age comes very softly on
like a door swung open, leading nowhere,
and a small wren lights on the rosemary bush,
    no heavier than a butterfly.

In the bowl of fruit on the chipped
enamel table, peaches speak,
lemons hum, and the day
    is just a *borgo* we belong to.

•

The poem bounces down the slope,
    a rock

you tossed and lost
found
    and threw away.

A bee flies by.

Each poem's not exactly what
    you mean
because, of course,
you don't
    quite ever know—

A bee returns.

•

Nearing the solstice, noon looms large.
    Trees and shrubs
suck their own shadows in.

    A hawk
cruises the fat slope and disappears
    over the ridge-crest.

Arrow of jay-flight,
    arc of the honeybees
humming where there are blossoms.

    The monastery gongs twelve times.
Astounding pine-smell
    brandished in narrow shade.

•

Sometimes I hear the bees,
    sometimes I see them.

More and more I suspect
        our perception slows and flattens the world
to get it inside our heads.

Suppose you had a sense
        tuned in to magnetism?
And one that could pick up quarks
        as they blink in and out
of what we call existence?

Somebody says that bees
        dance on a flag manifold,
interacting with quantum fields,
        speaking a language we can't conceive of.
Inside the hive is better than my head.

•

Rilke leans forward
to whisper a few
words to his Polish
translator, von Hulewicz.

Wir sind, he says,
able just for a moment
to think in six dimensions,
we are the bees of the invisible.

Bees are the bees
of the invisible, most likely.
But we are the ones
who get to think about it.

I'll take that home today,
high on this mountain,

high on the thoughts
that leave the words behind.

Bees on their patterned errands,
neutrinos on theirs,
pass right by and through us,
we, the big-brained dreamers.

•

We bought a round flat *crema* cake
    shaped like a moon
    in Umbertide.
It looks like a phosphorescent Frisbee.
We munch its wedges as the solstice turns.

The constellations wheel and quiver.
    All night, the small
    owls hoot and hunt,
skimming through pines,
and I slide down into the deeps and reefs

where humans go when they have lived too long—
    tangles of memory, imagination,
    animal faith and love,
the call of kin,
the missed and missing world.

•

These *tootings at the weddings
of the soul?* Well, one good sleight-of-hand
deserves another.

Solstice to solstice to solstice,
the yo-yo game around the sun,
stitching a life . . .

The great golden hive
of the invisible. Raw honey
and goat-footed sunlight.

Chopping Garlic

The bulb, an oriental palace
shrouded in gray-and-lavender paper,
splits open into a heap
of wedge-shaped packets housing
horns, fangs, monster toenails
all of a pungent ivory—I
could string them into a necklace
but I smash them flat instead,
loving the crunch, brushing away
all the confetti—clouds
of odor bloom around me now
as I chop, this way and that,
with my half-moon blade
in the scooped wood
that will never completely lose
the fragrance that oils it, smears
my fingers, wants to be in
the pores of my skin forever . . .
trumpets and cymbals blare
as I dump the grainy mess
into the pan, oh, holy to the nose
are the incense and sizzle that summon
folks from all parts of the house
to ask about dinner, sniffing,
while up in one end of the sky
a crescent moon hangs crazily,
a glowing clove,
a dangerous fragrance
filling the very corners
of some god's smiling mouth.

Dinner Time

Where a glass of red wine
glows on the sideboard

and a few potatoes in a dish,
floury, flecked with parsley,

shine in the taciturn dusk,
as voices are heard in the kitchen

through the noise of dishes and pots
while an old man in suspenders

holding a half-read newspaper
rubs a spoon on his shirt

holds it at arm's length
to catch his own reflection.

That Spring

The river was fast,
    icy vodka
    all through April.

It snowed, then rained—
    chicken-feathers, dust,
    confetti from another life.

The trees rose
    fervid as preachers,
    peopled with hymns.

Wind knocked some down,
    snapped others in half.
    The dead pine stood, and the wild cherries.

I made buffalo chili in the microwave
    and the light stood around
    longer every evening.

Sheep watched, distracted,
    as salesmen and Bible thumpers
    sailed past in limousines.

Thunder in a tall green bottle,
    lightning in a copper bowl,
    scattered in shards and pieces.

Tracks were seen in the mud,
      possum and squirrel, heron and crow,
      shiny and new in the half-light.

And one violin performed by itself,
      no violinist, not even a bow,
      the solo of a solo of a solo.

At the White Window

Whatever one sees beyond it—
green lawn, gray sky, blue heaving sea—

it's clear that the window's framing of the view
is half the meaning, maybe more.

The room is bare, the floorboards simple,
the sunlight falls in angles on the floor.

By being here alone, our sight
entering this picture, thoughtfully,

we celebrate both solitude and its mysterious
opposite, the sense of never being quite alone,

of having dim companions—from the past,
the future, from unsensed dimensions—

as we move slowly to the window,
never to raise the sash, or even touch the pane,

but simply to look out, acknowledging
our unabashed humanity, both frame and view.

The Snow Bird

Not a bird made of snow, but the snow itself—
snow is a bird.

Most of the feathers are unbelievably small,
lit from within.

Crisscrossing branches all through the woods
and the bird

falling among them, flying among them,
calling its no-call.

A squirrel scribbles the page of the yard.
The bird hides, white.

Falling by day, by night, needing no rest,
making the world its wing—

making the clouds its perch, the sweep and stitch,
the glare-hush . . .

Midwestern Families

Rummaging through drawers for socks and underwear,
    finding them full of little people—
    some lie there quietly,
    others thrash.

Possessions—a weathered house, a tipped barn,
    studs and cufflinks,
    the pond with its glowing images,
    slumped boots.

Your breath and my breath
    matched as we sleep,
    our slow hearts pumping
    the same soft thumps and swishes.

We never go wholly alone—
    the solitary bee, deep in the flower,
    is part of a restless colony,
    never quite absent.

The dish and the mirror ponder each other,
    the twister sings to itself in the distance,
    days pass, nights glitter,
    no one forgets the hymns.

Father picks up his pitted watch from the dresser,
    walks out in the cool morning . . .
    there stands a row of phantom little girls,
    hair-bows, starched pinafores, blinking.

Clouds flower slowly,
vermilion and saffron in the west,
while the moon rises, a white plate,
over fields of mesmerized wheat.

Phenomenology for Dummies

for Charles Simic

The blue lips of the sheriff,
the news of winter-killed rose plants,
remind me to finger your dreams,
their trees and wistful vistas,
the tables piled with food,
bottles of wine crying *Drink me!*

None of us has long, we hear,
and just so many poems left,
with more than enough dull moments
to sandwich in between.
Time to get up from the table,
take a stroll in the moonlight . . .

Soon enough, God knows,
everyone else will be asleep,
even the small-time demons,
while one of us will be sitting up,
next to a lamp and a moth,
keeping company with a book,
waiting for coffee and dawn.

Four Songs on a Bone Flute

1. SUMMER

This sprig of basil
out of my garden
teaches each sense—

green glow to light me
the way through the world
even the underworld

fragrance of summer
rough coasts and hills
baked in the sun

touched, it releases
even more odor
clouding my hands

flavor will hurry
all over my tongue
bursting horizons

and then there's the song
even more rousing
for making a silence.

2. FALL

"Wild poets of the north"
says the paper I happen

to hold in my hand
and amused
I swivel
to face the big lake
and the stacked clouds.

My sword's in the dust
which is where
it belongs.

All's lost, of course.
I sniff the air,
beaten, ready for winter.

3. WINTER

Part of you slept
safe in the dream-pen
part of you walked
to a door where you saw
a pathway of stars.

The night mind
and the night wind
were the same for a time.

Tonight when you
go to that
door you can nod
to the moon
once again
as she walks
east to west

in her white blouse
shedding it
wearing it,
wearing it
shedding it.

4.   SPRING

—*for my brother*

Mexico—we had climbed
to the temple ruin
and stood looking out
at present and past
not wanting to give either up.

We stopped at a shop.
I bought the blue cloth.

Women were beating
laundry and murmuring
down by the stream in the trees.

A church-bell rang slowly
boundaries vanished
the sun sprang up
the day was as if
it took in the full
wandering planet.

Light that remembers its origins.
Light from a very old source.

Lullaby for the Elderly

Under the hum and whir of night, under the covers, deep in the bed, beyond all the calling of doves, past the great flares of love and pain, the daily bread and grind, it's warm as a pot, soft as a breast. It's the deep woods, the place where you come to a clearing, find the still pool, and slip gently into it—to bathe, to dive, to drown.

Your mother is there, under the leaves, smelling of milk, and your father is hiding among the trees. A giant hand tousles your hair, and the mouse is there with its dangerous eyes, the bear with his shimmering fur, the rivers that thunder off ledges and spill into gorges as mist.

When you wake, refreshed, murmur a blessing for those who have never returned. Say a word to the corn and the wheat, to the deer and squirrels and whistling toads, who brought you right up to the edge of the woods and let you go in on your own.

The House Was Quiet on a Winter Afternoon

Someone was reading in the back,
two travelers had gone somewhere,
maybe to Chicago,

a boy was out walking, muffled up,
alert on the frozen creek,
a sauce was simmering on the stove.

Birds outside at the feeder
threw themselves softly
from branch to branch.

Suddenly I did not want my life
to be any different.
I was where I needed to be.

The birds swirled in the dusk.
The boy came back from the creek.
The dead were holding us up

the way the ice held him,
helping us breathe the way
air helps snowflakes swirl and fall.

And the sadness felt just right,
like a still and moving wave
on which the sun shone brilliantly.

from

Black Lab

Walking Around Retired in Ohio

After Lu Ji

I wake up at dawn these days,
called by an unknown voice,
heart racing,
get up and dress, then hesitate—

there isn't anywhere I have to go!

•

Think of a recluse, living in a gorge:
he spends a morning picking watercress,
sits on a hill to watch the sunset . . .

branches above him, clouds above the branches,
kingfisher green, kingfisher blue,
wind shouldering through honeysuckle,
and you lose yourself in fragrance . . .

the small creek bubbles, slightly pensive,
echoes back from the ridge . . .

•

Wealth is absurd and fame's a filthy habit.
People who chase these things are addicts.

Joy can't be faked, joy is just *there,*
was there all along, unscrolled itself
when you lost your urge to control
the many systems you would never master.

•

Get out of your car. Here's the Wildlife Preserve,
floating and humming with life.

The great big day, the new one.
Pines. Geese. A quizzical raccoon.

Weeds, clouds, birdsong, cicada buzz.
Now let the weather lead you. Walk!

Black Labrador

1.

Churchill called his bad visits from depression
a big black dog. We have reversed that, Winston.
We've named him Nemo, no one, a black hole
where light is gulped—invisible by night:
by day, when light licks everything to shine,
a black silk coat ablaze with inky shade.
He's our black lab, wherein mad scientists
concoct excessive energy. It snows,
and he bounds out, inebriate of cold.
The white flakes settle on his back and neck and nose
and make a little universe.

2.

It's best to take God backward; even sideways
He is too much to contemplate, "a deep,
but dazzling darkness," as Vaughan says.
And so I let my Nemo-omen lead me
onward and on toward that deep dark I'm meant
to enter, entertain, when my time comes . . .
The day wheels past, a creaky cart. I study
the rippling anthracite that steadies me,
the tar, the glossy licorice, the sable;
and in this snowfall that I should detest,
late March and early April, I'm still rapt
to see his coat so constellated, starred, re-starred,
making a comic cosmos I can love.

January 3, 2003

My father's breathing chugs and puffs and catches,
a slow train slowing further, rattling in
to its last stop, a locked and shuttered station.

Ninety-nine years this pair of lungs, this heart,
have done their work without complaint.
Time now to let them stop and draw their wages.

The years slide down a chute and disappear;
as memories dissolve and vaporize,
the body simplifies to mottled matter,

and if the myths have got it right for once,
he turns to find a welcome somewhere else,
to touch my mother's face and make her smile.

Putting My Father's Ashes in the Cemetery at Springville, Iowa

August 7, 2003

My brother and my sister shade their eyes
against the noonday glare. My cousins stroll
among the graves. These Grant Wood hills,
rich now with corn and soybeans,
seem to be just the place to set
this marble shoebox
deep in the earth, next to my mother's,
this earth that's full of relatives:
grandparents, uncles, aunts, the infants too,
some that lived long enough for names, some not,
each generation giving ground to others,
hidden and peaceful, like the family farms
down at the end of narrow shaded lanes
where tractors doze and trees stand tall and green
dreaming the summer into autumn.

At the Little Bighorn

It was October, there was steady drizzle,
small mice were nesting in the buckskin grass,
maybe a chicken hawk was cruising overhead,
or just a magpie posted on a fence . . .

I used to wonder why the Chinese poets
stopped off at battlefields, and mused, and wept,
picking up arrowheads and shattered halberds,
brushing quick poems on the hard-packed sand—

but I have been to Waterloo, and Gettysburg,
and come to think of it that beach in Normandy
named for the stockyard city I grew up in.
The great West, all those plains and badlands,

those miles of rye and soybean broken by a silo,
is neutral, sometimes, even to the magpies,
and maybe even mice can sense Wyoming
is mostly undulating empty prairie

and cloudscapes almost past conceiving.
Seeing the Tetons I couldn't quite believe
them, their weird beauty. It's slow work,
this hammering out our human world of spirit.

Christmas: Ohio and Capolungo

Like a soft doll the raptured angel lolls
above the dusty crèche; lights flicker
in all the downtown trees, while carols
crisscross the air from boxy speakers.

I'm in two places now: my country,
where the Nativity is clumsy but familiar,
and that inept museum, east of Nervi,
which shows me crèches of another order:

elaborate pageants, carefully arranged,
all lace and straw and flat-out piety,
the underside of what made art both strange
and wonderful, that Catholic sense of deity.

We're never going to get God right. But we
learn to love all our failures on the way.

Eating a Red Haven Peach in the Middle of August in Ohio

I'm having a tingle, a kind of
Wanda Landowska moment here,
as my senses converge on this fruit and the sun
rests a warm palm on my back and neck
and just for a moment I don't even mind
the bad news I've been hearing, reading,
the little daily shit storm, constant rain of lies,
the President's moral hairspray,
the weeds that riot through my herbs,
the distances to China and Peru.
                                    They say

biting a fruit cost us our chance
to stay in Paradise? Well, Eve, old thing,
this peach, this perfume turned to wine
and all-out fuzzbound sweetness
just sent me back there for a moment.

Dawn on the Winter Solstice

The way day inches up, off to the south,
grudging the world even a night-light's glow,
recalls an empty shop, its goods ransacked.

A day with a catch in its throat,
maybe a sob. Maybe a marsh
freezing slowly, like an empty dance floor.

The wind, that blowhard, has retired,
leaving us just the rolled steel cold
that chills our tears, fixes our angry smiles.

Seventeen starlings are desperately
searching an old lady's driveway
in case there are crumbs to fight for,

as the year groans on its hinge
and I start to hum for it all
since somewhere else, I think,

in a time and place much like this
my mother is teaching me carols
at a modest piano, next to an evergreen.

Faux Pas

The fox paused at the field's edge, paw raised,
looked back and switched her tail, the way
a thrush will flutter among maple leaves—
that's when I thought of you, choosing
your words, taking your careful steps,
sleeping so restlessly.
Our distance is not so much miles
as years and memories, mine such leafy compost
I shake my head, too full of duff and humus
to get a bearing or a fix. Foxfire, that weird
by-product of wood-decay, pulses in me today . . .
And look: after the vixen left, trailing a faint rank scent,
a freight passed slowly, flatcars in mizzling rain,
some of them loaded with truck trailers, some not,
objects that no more need attention than you need
waste time upon my lurching, coupled feelings.
Go with the fox—I send a sort of blessing
as gulls lift off the reservoir and day,
a spreading bruise against the western rim,
drains January and the freshened year.

Sally and the Sun

Thus we understand "cut" in the sentences "The barber cut my hair," "The tailor cut the cloth," and "The surgeon cut the skin" quite differently because we bring to bear on these sentences a large cultural background knowledge . . . For the same reason we don't know how to interpret the sentences "Sally cut the sun" or "Bill cut the mountain."

—JOHN SEARLE, *The New York Review of Books*

1.
Sally cut the sun,
Billy cut the mountain;
Andy had some fun
At the soda fountain.

Ruby caught the light—
No one told her not to;
Janice was a fright
After she'd been taught to.

Diamond cut the glasses,
Jesus cut the cheese;
Goat-boy cropped the grasses
Nodding in the breeze.

2.
Sally cut the sun,
Then she cut the moon;
She was carving paper
During the monsoon.

Billy cut the mountain,
Then it had a notch.

Sun went down behind it.
Billy drank some scotch.

Daniel handled language,
John observed him closely;
Breakfast was an anguish,
Dinner also, mostly.

Cyril toasts his mother,
Crystal coats a sleeve;
Talking with another
Makes me start to grieve.

Rose inside the iceberg,
Ice inside the rose.
Billy kisses Sally,
Sally breaks his nose.

Bill clear-cut the mountain.
Then it was all stumps.
Sally cut the sunlight,
Then she got the mumps.

Watch the phoenix rise
Perfect from its ashes,
Rigid with surprise,
Circled round with flashes.

Blake's "Dante and Virgil Penetrating the Forest" (1824)

The trees are full of life, streamlined and shapely;
their leaves are blobs and networks, rising water,
and everything is bluish-green, as if
this whole scene were submerged.

The two men, shapely too, have one strong contrast:
the younger poet's arms are at his sides,
palms out, a gesture of rejection.

Virgil, however, holds both arms aloft,
not just referring to the forest but
by being treelike, even more than Dante,
he's saying, Blake insists,
We are the forest!

It is not other, it is what we are!
The trees lean in to listen and agree.

Late Celan Variations

WURFSCHEIBE, mit
Vorgesichten besternt,

wirf dich

aus dir hinaus.

1.
THROWPLATE, with
a face full of stars and foresights

throw yourself

out of yourself.

2.
THROWNDISC
starred with ancestor faces,

throw thyself

out of thyself.

3.
DISCUS, starred
with prehistoric things to come

go
throw

yourself
out.

4.
FRISBEE,
premonition-constellated—

spin right on

out of yrself,

5.
NIGHTSKY, you discus,
stellate with foreseeings,

toss

thyself

away.

6.
BIGBANG, a mix
of faces, warnings, stars,

finish it

be the Big
Crunch.

February 1, 2003

The tiny spacecraft twists and burns, exploding
against the friction of the atmosphere,
raining small pieces over Texas.

If you could ride the tall auroras
dancing above the Pole, perhaps
you could exempt yourself from pain?

Oh wrap this up in language, quick,
so I can bear it. Talk about Icarus or Phaeton,
tell stories of our origins and hopes.

Grape-colored sky at evening—
the mind walks numbly over windblown acres
picking up tiles, fragments, chunks.

Walking Home on an Early Spring Evening

Every microcosm needs its crow,
something to hang around and comment,
scavenge,
alight on highest branches.

Who hasn't seen the gnats,
the pollen grains that coat the windshield—
who hasn't heard the tree frogs?

In the long march that takes us all our life,
in and out of sleep, sun up, sun gone,
our aging back and forth, smiling and puzzled,
there come these times: you stop and look,

and fix on something unremarkable,
a parking lot or just a patch of sumac,
but it will flare and resonate

and you'll feel part of it for once,
you'll be a goldfinch hanging on a feeder,
you'll be a river system all in silver
etched on a frosty driveway, you'll

say "Folks, I think I made it this time,
I think this is my song." The crow lifts up,
its feathers shine and whisper,

its round black eye surveys indifferently
the world we've made
and then the one we haven't.

I Wear My Father

I've made his amber aftershave last out
through this whole year of missing him;
I wear my father's cardigan.
I swear I'm turning into him,

saying "Yupyupyup" to the puppy
as I bend to leash him, breathing harder,
pursing my lips as memories crowd my head,
settling my hat on firmly as I leave.

The other day, though, on the icy creek,
as a heron rose up from a crosswise trunk
I slipped and slid against the snowy bank,
cracked through the ice sheet, up to one knee.

The dog looked rightly puzzled. As for Dad,
he'd not have been that dumb, I tell myself,
making my aging foolishness keep me
younger, somehow, and singular.

Chloe in Late January

Midwinter here, a frozen pause, and now
some nineteen years since cancer took your life.

This month's old god, they say, faced opposite directions,
backward and forward. May I do that too?

It's much the same. Deer come and go, as soft
as souls in Hades, glimpsed at wood's edge toward dusk;
their tracks in daylight show they come at night
to taste my neighbor's crab trees, last fall's fruit
shrunk down to sour puckered berries.

And where, in this arrested world,
might I expect to meet your cordial spirit?

You would not bother with that graveyard, smooth
below its gleaming cloak of snow. You'd want
to weave among the trees, beside the tiny kinglet,
gold head aglow, warming itself
with ingenuities, adapting, singing,
borne on the major currents of this life
like the creek that surprised me yesterday again,
running full-tilt across its pebbled bottom
even in this deep cold.

The Secret Life of Light

1.
Reading *The Secret Life of Dust*,
learning about
the "wispy disk" of cosmic dust
that circulates around the sun and that
"on rare occasions you can see
a glowing slice of this
'zodiacal light,' "
described by an astronomer
named G. Cassini, 1683,
I realize that I've seen it!

Way out above the sea, a shining wedge
we couldn't figure out as we came down
at dusk from our big climb
to Santa Croce.

We were so lost and tired that our view,
the *Golfo Paradiso* all spread out
from Genoa to Portofino Mountain,
made hardly any sense,
although we had to venerate the sea
a sheet of hammered metal
in mute and muting light
as we stepped down the path
as carefully as pack mules,
hurrying to get back
to where we'd have
our bearings once again
before the dark closed in.

David, you said the odd
inverted pyramid with blurry corners

might be a UFO. Janine and I
thought it was some strange opening in clouds.
Well, now we know, we pilgrims,
who had been past the Stations of the Cross
going and coming, and had talked about
the pious folk who climbed up on their knees
on special days, at dawn,
up to that little church
that stands so high and barren . . .

2.

Now we know what? That in a world
where superhuman meanings have been drained
we take our best encounters with the things
that are not human, don't belong to us,
the "zodiacal light" just one more sign
that points back to itself, or at the best
to its own cosmic history:
our origins in dust,
that cloud that once congealed
enough to form a star
that then became our sun
and then helped form the earth
and still rains down around us,
still lights up the sky,
a burning golden triangle
around the equinox
above the sea beyond
the port of Genoa.

Comets go past, and we don't notice,
asteroids just miss us by two moon lengths,
the sun burns on, throwing gigantic flares and flowers,
we fill our eyes and word-hoards,
pick our way down mule trails,

and trust that somehow we belong to this,
the life of secret dust,
and it makes sense, somehow.

I might have spoken to that glow.
"Oleh," I might have said. *"Grandfather."*
I might have fallen to my knees, for once.
Ashes to ashes. Secret life. And dust
and light, a little light,
is maybe all we have?

    3.
I think I'd like to write
The Sacred Life of Dust,
but I don't have the means.
Parked along a back road,
I'm jotting all this down
on old prescription pads
and one much-crumpled shopping list,
a January day,
the sun a dimming disk;
the radio is offering
the best thing that could happen,
Das Musikalische Opfer,
Bach's canons that perform
like crabs, mirrors, comets,
and I'll go on about my errands now,
something for our dinner,
something from the pharmacy.

A blue jay soars up to an apple branch
in one unfolding movement
and I look on in shock,
as if I'd never seen
a living thing that flies!

Part of me stays on earth,
part of me rises with the jay.

The day rolls forward toward
the secret life of dusk.

The Dream of the Moving Statue

Nothing much, and little else.
We had a lot of rooms to visit. Nothing simple.

We used a flashlight just to get around
the huge and cluttered building. No one spoke.

Clusters of trash and funny echoes;
something that moved ahead of us, a rat,

maybe a bat or one small roosting owl.
I hummed a tune that was inaudible

and you, you seemed morose, remembering
dead family members, pets you'd lost . . .

Well, nobody got hurt and no one minded
the pastness of the past, its growing distance.

This was the sort of thing we did at night,
often while sleeping, sometimes when awake.

Yoshitoshi

The flute-players, two men, face each other. The virtuoso prince, his back to us, wears a strange peaked cap. The foreigner, whose beard and costume give him away (Mongolian?), faces us. His eyes are downcast as he concentrates on his playing.

The prince's robe is olive-green. White, purple, and red chrysanthemums, widely spaced, make up its ornamentation. The foreigner's robe is lavender. A bright red under-robe shows below. In the silence of the scene, costume and garb must replace the unheard music.

They are next to some kind of monumental gate. Is the virtuoso teaching? Welcoming a visitor? Is this duet a habit or an accident?

This prince is said to be so gifted that once, when he had been robbed, the sound of his flute in response to his loss made the thieves repent and return what they had taken.

The full moon takes it in and gives it back. The flutists almost float, like ghosts, in its disinterested sea. They mirror each other, playing together, silent and concentrated, alike within their differences. The moon will wax and wane, always the same because it is always changing.

March 10, 2001

Three crisscrossed daffodils
faint lamps in the rubble

where without any warning
I'm shattered by your absence

wondering will I always
blunder into this emotion

so large and mute it has no name
—not grief longing pain

for those are only its suburbs
its slightly distracting cousins—

summoned just now by these
frilled blossoms

butter yellow horns
on lemon yellow stars

indifferent innocent
charging in place

advance guard of a season
when I will join you.

Swithin

Inside my dream the fair-haired ancient saint
who visited a group of living friends
gathered together in an English cottage

walked without stepping, read our thoughts,
spoke without need to use his mouth,
shone with a glow that didn't hurt the eyes,

moved among those he blessed
smiling a riveting smile,
and felt, when he came to hug me,

not like another body but
not immaterial either, since
his fragrance was amazing.

When I was left alone in that dim room,
stroking a smoky cat and musing,
my mind charged up with wonder and relief,

it didn't seem to me I'd been "converted"
but it did seem I'd had a glimpse of something
that would remember me when I forgot it.

The Hour of Blue Snow

Dusk on these late winter days
is a matter of daylight giving a little shrug,
then vanishing.

But when it does, the blue snow moment comes.

That's when, for instance, two or three deer
materialize from nowhere, stroll through the back yard,
and vanish in the woods. As when the ancient gods
came down to wander their enchanted world.

Then I remember to breathe again,
and the blue snow shines inside me.

March 2005

New Poems (2010)

Why I Translate

You lived in bad times,
Du Mu, and you
almost never complained.

What was your secret?
Crabwise, I try to edge my way
inside your life.

Someone
just hurried
through the village.

•

Out on the river, drifting,
the man becomes the river,
the current full of thoughts.

•

Memories are bees;
at best, in season,
they have a hive to go to.

•

The ice is breaking up. The sun
is brilliant now, and light
spreads through the budding trees.

•

Bad times, good times, and the world goes on.
The heart rises, a large bird,
cruising in evening air.

And the river moves through everything.

The Merry-Go-Round

To be stretched out forever,
floating in full gallop,

to have the bright-red saddle fused
always to the smooth white back,

to be impaled, with a slow rise and fall,
on one long gleaming pole . . .

no wonder the teeth are bared,
the eyes wild and bright,

as if to say, unheard, unlistened to,
bad art! bad art! bad art!

Mother's Day

—for my children

I see her doing something simple, paying bills,
or leafing through a magazine or book,
and wish that I could say, and she could hear,

that now I start to understand her love
for all of us, the fullness of it.

It burns there in the past, beyond my reach,
a modest lamp.

Quick Takes

Traveling upstream again
with the peeled sycamores lit up,
dumbfounded by the seasons.

•

Bocca, que ditz?
Thus Arnaut Daniel, and then Pound:
"Mouth, now what knacks!"

•

The pine grew fragrant as I stood beside it
just as the sun grew stronger.
In the breeze, the smell of other trees.

•

And in the sky, the constellation Rabbit,
hanging in the east, askew,
as if I had not just invented it!

•

Faint dawn, pale apricot, pale lime,
and the owl sails silent to his roost . . .
the history of the earth would be my gospel.

•

So there you walk, and language is your shadow,
stretching ahead when you are lucky,
more often trailing behind.

•

Margaret pregnant, expecting in March,
and I recall T's words:
"two hearts kicking inside her."

•

Good days, bad days,
telling them apart,
then shuffling them, a deck of cards.

•

There's my gone father, back again:
the stopped train, the close-grained oak,
the swinging, flashing mirror.

One Hundred Billion Neurons in My Brain

I counted them,
right after counting all the stars
that constitute the Milky Way—
same number.

Okay, I'm kidding.
I lost count.

Someone was making waves, and someone else
was summoning storms.

When materialism's much
more mystery-filled than mystery,
what do we say or do?

That matter
matters?

I'm told that to count the synapses
would take me up around five hundred *trillion*.

But, brain, counting aside,
you've not worked hard enough.
Once again, old cauliflower,
you've loafed your way through an assignment.

Mind your own body now, okay?

Use your two sides
to balance what I think, do, feel.

And please, keep dreams in check,
both when you wake and sleep,

you blend of sparks and giddiness,
you bowl of blood and thunder,
you three-pound fist of spam and hope-maps,
snuggled inside your helmet bone
making your moves and movies.

Occasional Sonnets

1. POLITICIANS INTERVENING IN THE TERRI SCHIAVO CASE

I read that Freud, after his visit here in 1909,
remarked that America was a mistake.
A large and interesting mistake, but a mistake.
Jesus, he's right, I think, and slap my brow,

ashamed, once more, to be American,
to list our history of bonehead deeds,
our deadly spread across the continent,
our huge addiction for hypocrisies . . .

But then I think, Well, what was Germany?
And England? France? Austria and the rest?
At least we tried some new stuff, and

sometimes behaved as if we could be different.
What is a nation? Something fairly lethal.
Put down that flag and take a good long walk.

2. VINIO ROSSI

d. Aug. 12, 2005

A large spirit, and a grave and funny heart.
And maybe now he can go back to France
and, when he wants to wander, on to Italy,
to sit out by some river, like the Po:

small table, glass of red wine, breathing,
dish of risotto, fragrant with porcini . . .

the day, reflected idly in the river,
takes on a certain majesty, a scope;

clouds build above it, and it's then you sense
an afterlife may not go on forever;
there is a touch of autumn in the air.

Seasons for the dead as well, then. Day will close
with an elemental sunset, and the night
will step forth in an armature of stars.

3.   THE VOID

Baudelaire, "Le Gouffre"

Pascal's great void was always next to him.
But everything's abyss! Desire, act, and dream,
language itself! My hair will rise and stand,
as I sense fear within the passing wind.

Above, below, all round—depths and vacuity:
silence and space attract me as they terrify . . .
Deep in my nights God's clever, moving hand
traces out nightmares I can't understand.

Sleep is no good, it's like a drop-off, giant,
peopled with horrors, plunging, bottomless . . .
Infinity peers in my windows, rapt,

and all my vertigo-torn spirit wants
is the idiotic bliss of Nothingness:
but numbers and existence keep me trapped!

4. READING YANNIS RITSOS IN NOVEMBER

A basket of apples, a bunch of carrots,
a poppy recognized as summer's wristwatch . . .
Sunlight and suffering, the old Greek way—
the new one too—did not desert him;

in prison, out of it, he drew and mused and wrote,
cherished small things that never went away,
and dreamed a revolution too, that never came,
the lit mirage of a just and ordered city.

Here in Ohio snow will be falling,
and I'm back to a night in 1957,
walking out of a dorm in Minnesota

and seeing northern lights across the heavens,
banners and shimmering folds of green and rose,
indifferent to our wondering, upturned faces.

5. WALT WHITMAN SMOOTHING THE FOREHEAD OF
   GERARD MANLEY HOPKINS

So different these two men, their worlds unsettled,
a civil war, the slums of Liverpool,
one struggling as a priest and one a roustabout,
and yet they come together in two passions:

the force of poetry, the way it takes them over,
and loves of their same gender, much denied them.
So I've convened them, sitting by a lamp,
handing each other poems, scribbled sheets

with crossings-out and underlinings, question marks
coiling in the margins, exclamation points—
they are not *thinking,* they are *making poems,*

bold enough, and crazy, stretching language,
a heaving tenderness, to bring their voices
into our ears, we whom they've loved too.

6. THE DEAD FROM IRAQ

They come back and stand in our midst,
young men in camouflage, heads shaved,
with undecided smiles, puzzled eyes.
We seldom happen to perceive them—

partly because we never really wish to;
vague sentinels, stiff at attention,
there in the corners of our vision
among the reeds or trees or graves.

This morning, as the season shifts again,
I'm more morose, half-conscious of their presence,
their numbers and their distribution,

real and not real, somber and too silent,
like phantom limbs that, after amputation,
we slowly talk ourselves out of using.

7. STAN SMITH

My cousin Stan is dead at ninety,
who fought on Okinawa—never said
what that was like, wounded and then shipped home.
Too much discrepancy between those places:

Iowa, where he farmed and auctioned cattle,
and those green jungles and long beaches
where death was everyday and human blood
seemed to be smeared and sprayed on everything . . .

Today, in this Ohio, like his Iowa,
the local woods were carpeted with bluebells
and in the meadow they surrounded, bluebirds.

Nature's own color scheme, I think.
Blues for Stan Smith. Some piercing sorrow, yes,
but who can argue with such destinies?

Reasons for Living

There aren't that many, surely.
A tiny, crumpled list
you keep in purse or wallet.

Meanwhile, though,
think of your life as a bulky
present you were given
sometime around your first birthday.

You spend your years unwrapping it, perhaps.

Or you finish unwrapping, discover it's a kit,
and spend your years assembling it.

The directions, if that is what they are,
are too confusing, with lots of gaps,
and there are way too many parts.

What you finally manage to put together
may or may not be what the kit intended,
but it's yours, like a pet you never planned to own;
even if you run out of reasons to live,
it expects your care and maintenance.

Poem at Seventy

Rick went to Shanghai and was invited
     to meet the "stomach talker," a spirit named *Lingge*
     in an otherwise unremarkable young woman
who spoke like a three-year-old
     but had been "everywhere in the world"
and knew "most languages."

He asked should he be fearful for his children.
     She said *Do not be worried, just concerned.*

He asked her why there was a universe.
     She said, *That was just Nature's way.*

He went away skeptical . . . and much intrigued.

And when he told me about it
     I remembered 1968, in London,
when we went to hear a medium,
     Robert Bly and Michael Benedikt and I,

an ordinary middle-aged lady
     who stood at a podium, as if to read some poems
or give a talk on politics or quilting
     and she got "messages" for people in the audience.

She saw the auras round our heads and she saw spirits
     who she said signaled to us, holding up tokens—
watches, violins, wedding rings.

I went away impressed and wondering
     but later thought the whole thing rather silly,
a net of weaved belief, made by those present,

especially those who'd suffered loss and wished to know
their dead were peaceful and forgiving.

All of those tokens were clichés.

I asked my wife if I might take her grieving father there
and she said, *Absolutely not!*

•

Everyone *knows* that something lies beyond us,
something that just escapes our senses,
there's a shadow, there's a luminescence,
a music we can nearly hear, a nimbus . . .

Sounds come over sometimes, tingling,
glimpses are granted at the edge of sleep,
a voice that seems to call our name, a deep
flash of sudden understanding . . .

The ordinary world lights up, a dance,
its thick distractions fall away,
and you're continuous with everything.

You can be wild, knowing this, and sing;
you can be matter-of-fact and day-to-day.
Your mood makes little difference.

•

Rick and I did *qigong* on the terrace
on a summer morning, listening to a tape,
and I was part of what was all around me:
the hummingbirds that came and went

deep in the giant honeysuckle bush,
the squirrel that trotted on a downed tree-limb,
the catbird skimming past me, shoulder-high,
the wild cherry trees rising toward the clouds.

This was no mystical experience, just pleasure
at being outside on a day in June.
all senses open, body moving at its ease.

No need for mediums or stomach talkers.
"Dancing with the Rainbow"—"Looking at the Moon"—
"Wheeling with the Millwheel"—"Scooping up the River."

·

When whippoorwills call
and evening is nigh,
I hurry to
My
Blue
Heaven.

Hölderlin stumbles home . . .
he's walked, somehow,
from Bordeaux back to Swabia.

His sanity is much in question.

Apollo did this to him.

·

At seventy now, I seem to be filled with voices,
scraps of the past, night shade,
blown visions, questions,
the touch of past parlayers, poets, friends.

As if I'm a vessel that must soon pour out
my brimming contents, lose them
in the air or in the earth,
wherever they end up, or don't,

and let my husk be empty. Out there
I sense my father sometimes, mother too,
and reigning, queen of the night, my Chloe,

who "sang beyond the genius of the sea . . ."
who let me be myself and sing
beyond the ruffled confines of the lake.

•

The baby's fist
curls round your finger
and the world goes buzzing on its way.

The baby stares around itself,
taking the world in with amazement,
or so it seems. And then it turns back to the breast.

That's what we'd like: two nourishments,
the mother's breast,
the lit, amazing world.

And the common sense, or fundamental sense,
not to confuse the two,
one human, one more-than-human.

Margaret nurses Quentin

and I am utterly content.

•

I fly to London, dozing far above
the heaving, cold Atlantic.

No medium this time,
no Robert and no Michael, no Chloe or her dad.

I will pace thoughtfully by Hawksmoor's churches,
admiring how they managed to combine

sheer heavy matter, stone, with soaring spirit,
back in those days of chaos laced with vision,

as in my old friend Henry Vaughan,
poets like Milton and Marvell,

and some of that time's music,
Baroque and all it meant, no going back,

Purcell and Handel, lifting up in song,
soaring toward what . . .

•

Analogies sail through, comparisons
for states and visions I can't name:

Like a woodpecker on a picnic blanket

Maybe I just like the music of it?

Like Varya's little dog, next to her wooden leg.

No, now it's more than just its sounds
for Varya now exists and since
wooden leg and woodpecker

came along by accident together
a narrative begins, a false one . . .

Varya's picnic . . .

This struggle to express, bound up
with vanity and ego, appetite for praise,
all fairly useless.

•

But December rolls around, I have a birthday, cook a meal.
The nights are dark and long
and filled with owls.

And the solstice, as I said to Franz,
the solstice always moves me

because I love this planet so.

Love this planet "mightily," I said,
thinking of its size and great variety.

By candlelight
we face each other
at the winter solstice.

•

So the planet's tilt once more
begins to face the sun, bringing it back.

A winter walk, bleak sunshine.

The woods are silent,
the reservoir is frozen,
nothing is stirring in the cornfield.

The low light bounces here and there
off cornstalks, off the ice-rimmed rocks,
and tells me
not to lose
my sense of warp and woof.

·

When Rilke came to visit me, around the time
he would have been one hundred, I thought then
that he seemed very tall.
                    That might have been
because I was lying on the floor.
                              You will say
this must have been a dream, hallucination,
something of that sort. You may be right,
but oh how clearly I remember him, tall Rilke!

·

We want to make things that will outlast us,
we humans, we can't seem to help that,
it's an instinct.

Facing my own death, maybe coming sooner
than I thought,
I think of how I might live on:

in my children and grandchildren,
in my students and my friends,
and in my poems, even my translations.

And I see this doesn't matter!
Not a bit!
And yet it's what I've done, assiduous me,

building up a store of me, a bunch of rooms,
where I may still survive,
a friendly ghost,

among my fading artifacts. "This living hand,"
Keats wrote.
It reaches out to touch you.

Oh turn away! Your own life
is what you should be living.
Mine is gone. And as I say, it doesn't matter!

Graveyard

Here on the stones there are words and numbers;
age has rubbed some of them to faintness.

Names and dates, they mingle with the grass,
the oaks and acorns, clouds and sky above.

Does that conjunction make all this, I wonder,
a sort of mute, gigantic poem?

Stones lean, birds pass, light settles.
Nobody speaks and nobody even listens.

I kneel to brush some twigs and leaves
and make your three names visible.

Three names, two dates, a pinecone:
a small stone page of the world's great book.

Stone I could put my head on, sleep,
and drift like a boat into the distance.

New Poems II (2022)

Quantum Haiku

1.

My black Lab, Nemo,
dead three years, half-forgotten,
just nosed my elbow.

2.

That sidewalk leaf-stain
on this bright April morning?
Hopkins in profile.

3.

Ten billion planets
in this galaxy alone—
we *think* we matter.

4.

She crosses my mind—
flame of the candle flickers
without any breeze.

5.

The snow was falling
like snow falling. No other
way to—then it stopped.

6.
Cooks? "Who *looks* for you?"
is what the owl calls these days;
the answer: no one.

7.
Galileo sees
all the moons of Jupiter—
now we're a planet!

8.
Crossing with Charon
Orfeo takes the punt-pole:
Hell's never the same.

9.
Chopin mazurka.
Self-portrait of my double:
Darwin shakes his head.

10.
My window's open.
Keats: "The poet has no self."
Bee-swarm on a chair.

11.
Wild bounty indeed.
Phone sex with a vampire.
Yielding as a cloud.

12.
I was the scarecrow
watching the boxcars roll past.
head full of straw-brains.

13.
Earth is a death-fest—
we need to get used to that:
the elk's antlers branch.

Her Voice Has Vanished

1.

Summer dusk, in Omaha, 1946;
children are outside, playing Kick the Can,
and I'm among them. Locusts sizzle in the trees,
and one by one the streetlights will blink on.

War is over. We beat the Japanese and Germans.
I have a baby brother. Soon, my mother
will summon me and I will go to bed and sleep
and drift all night through jungle Okinawas.

The August moment in itself is nothing,
neither then, nor now as I recall it.
The planet shudders, though, as if

with sudden happiness, responding to
that moment, nothing else behind, ahead,
only the summer dusk and playing children.

2.

Her voice floats on the mild air. "David,"
it calls. I hear it and respond. Children and dusk,
and mothers calling, among the oldest things,
one of the sounds that give the summer meaning.

Meaning and fullness. Call me again, dear one,
call from wherever you are. I'll come.
We'll be together in the summer dusk,
the ripening of time. I'll take your hand.

Nothing is permanent. No one should pretend
time can be anything other than water,
something that slips through hands and fingers.

No one should ask the past for help, or comfort,
no one should try to resist the deep snows
that help us understand why summer ends.

Pacing Around in the Memory Palace

It's Guy Fawkes Day, 1983.
Chloe and Margaret take the train
from London to the Lake District
to meet me there.
                    As evening spreads,
they see the village bonfires, near and far,
flares in the darkening landscape.

Chloe is dying, Margaret is growing up.
They share the magic of this moment
while I, because I did not travel with them,
attempt to share it each November, missing it,
and recreating it as best I can.

That's how memory behaves, rewarding you
and holding back, both ways at once,
as bittersweet as anything
when you grow tired of bitter, tired of sweet.

Reading Old Letters on a Rainy Morning

If it could eat us up, it would, the past.

But it is old and toothless, mostly,
or helpless as a baby. We can visit,
but we can turn away, oblivious,
preoccupied with present mind and body.

Between my thumb and finger
I hold the cable that I sent to London
some forty-seven years ago,
announcing my son's birth.

An artifact as precious as a potsherd.

Ephemeral may simply mean *immortal*.

What this was then seems clear enough. But what
does it mean now? I watch the morning rain
run down the window like an unknown language.

Watching My Grandson Play
Mamillius in *The Winter's Tale*

Lenox, Mass., 8/15/2010

These stories with their old and silly plots
whose meaning it may take you a whole life
to comprehend: how loss is always loss
and always also restoration—how
winter is spring, and even death gives life.

It's nearly forty years since I first wrote
about this play. I understood it, partly.
Time says, "I turn my glass," and I knew what
that meant, a choric trick of sorts:
both literal (his hourglass), and then
as one deft figure for the play itself:
a tragedy, when Time turns upside down,
finds itself mirrored in a comedy.

And now this curtain call. Mamillius,
whom we all know was dead and can't return,
dashes out first to take a smiling bow:
he's not Mamillius, he's Colin Young,
and we, as one, are rising to our feet
as tears run down a host of weathered faces.

Nothing is lost. And everything is lost.
It takes a foolish plot, a statue come to life,
to teach us this, and touch us, till we laugh
and cry, and shake our heads again, in wonder.

Heidelberg Beach, October

1.
Lake Erie stretched out and shining
and once again, the sunset,
leaving me speechless.

2.
I know, it isn't the sun setting,
it's the earth turning away,
neither of them worried
by the details of their intimacy.

3.
The heron on the dock
turns its head slowly
as if to remind me
we're gifted, both, to be part of it:
the traveling light,
traveling light.

Value and Reverie

The dog dreams on the rug
legs twitching slightly
and in his dream, I think,
he trots through a puddle,
breaking up the sky.

It's like a lament that has
been set to music, sung
so beautifully that,
though still a lament,
it lifts the sorrow into joy,

while early October sunlight
slides through grass and leaves
and the dog wakes up
rolls on his stomach
nose pushed forward like a boat
wags his tail once, and sighs.

August Notes

1. TOMAS TRANSTRÖMER

I fell asleep naked in my bed.
In sleep I was helpless, and safe.

I dreamed of a tree, roots and crown,
I dreamed of the tide moving in.

In my dream I rushed forward toward death
and was joyous, naked, and safe.

2. IS THE SELF LIKE A FLOCK OF BIRDS?

The gulls fly past, fifteen together,
just a few feet above smooth Lake Erie.

They are like one large creature,
made up of fragments, coherent in movement.

And we are fragments too, of time and feeling,
loosely joined in this morning sun.

3. BAUDELAIRE AND HIS CORRESPONDENCES

As if you were a camera, roaming
dim deserted hospital corridors.

As if the meteors, brighter than tear-tracks,
flashed each August across night sky.

As if that big hawk, flushed near dusk,
from the trees that line the field . . .

Basho

Each poem is a tiny door,
or better still,
a window.

Light as a snowflake,
slippery as a whale,
poised as a candle,
silent as an orchid.

We've walked a long way together.
Somewhere ahead of us
a horse whinnies,
a crow calls,
a beetle's becoming a firefly.

The horse and the crow are a poem.

The firefly lights our way.

Herman Melville Feeding His Chickens

We all have dreams that leave us stunned and speechless.

We have routines that bring us back to earth,
to sun and fine May mornings, stretching out
like recollections of a blue and rolling ocean.

We all have secrets and deep memories.

Scatter the grain in graceful arcs. Now go
back to your desk, sharpen your pen, and write
a monstrous novel. Who's going to stop you?

There is no god. There is a god.
Both sentences are true.

Paul Celan by Starlight

Celan is outside looking at the stars.
He does this often, pacing off his pain
and gazing upward, letting his great bitterness
stream out through galaxies and constellations.

A dog barks somewhere in the distance.
The past's a horror, the future is its mirror,
but in this moment, under a midnight sky,
there is a gap of perfect emptiness.

Chilly and hopeless, he mines a line of verse.
Not that the stars give comfort. It is more
that their indifference is what he needs,
so he can bear to handle simple words.

Baudelaire, The Cats

Both steamy lovers and ascetic scholars
Are equally attached, as they grow old,
To cats—soft, cruel, the household's rulers,
Lazy and idle, sensitive to cold.

Friends both to science and to sensual pleasure,
They seek out silence and Horror's darkness;
The Devil might have made them pull his treasure
If they could be persuaded into harness.

They often doze assuming noble poses
Resembling the great sphinxes, old and wise,
Dreaming an endless dream, so one supposes.

Their fertile loins are full of sparks, it seems,
And particles of gold, sand grains of dreams,
Add mystic galaxies within their eyes.

January 28

Today it is snowing again and I'm thinking of Borges.
Something he understood is floating abroad.
It's a garden of forking paths, a lottery, a library,
a room where Funes still lies in the dark,
lost in his reverie.

Dream-wise, the snow comes down . . .

I met the man once, admired
his unseeing face, his simple composure
gazing inside at what we so seldom glimpse,
the endless ocean of human suffering.

The snow rims every branch, each twig;
each field's a white expanse,
a page of forgotten light.

Since Galileo Started Something

1.

Now that our microcosm's been scaled down
to subatomic particles

while macrocosm is scaled up
to take in galaxy behaviors,

maybe we need John Donne again
to help us with extremes?

I sift a handful of his dust
into the LHC* , and listen for results.

Did he say "dark matter"?
Did he say "multiverse"?

Did he say "Hadron"?
Or was it "Hard-on"?

Did he say Higgs? Did he say boson?
God particle? Bring back the Mass?

The interaction was too weak.
Communication with deep time

is harder than deep space,
but we can try again.

* Large Hadron Collider

2.

Let scale go back today to what's familiar,
the cabbage butterfly on the clover blossom,

the butterfly white, the blossom rose-magenta,
the woods around them, rising, rising green,

and let us wander in and out of knowledge.
Haven't we all the time in the world?

"Edge, Rim, Frontier, Limit"

The frame of the poem, out at the edge,
is where you surely need to be.

The foreground's good, of course,
the background has its charms,
but in the end you need those borders:

the title you came in through,
white margins left and right,
and then the close, the end, that place
where poem stops and you, forsooth, resume,
already wondering what it meant to you,
and whether you should go back through
or put it all behind you.

In this case you can say
the whole thing was a trick, a playful thing
that left you puzzling on a slippery surface:

the framing title, framed itself by quote marks,
the poem, self-contained, autonomous,
a little smug, leaving you out
or letting you go on, at last.

A Valediction Discounting Sorrow

I take off the world, a little at a time.

I remove my gigantic shoes.
I take off my shirt of water.

A door creaks, it is the ants,
coming to tell me their story.

Trees bloom and leaf, but mainly in the memory.

Clouds shadow us as we go downhill,
happy to be moving freely.

I take off the weight of houses, walls,
the sorrow of floors and ceilings.

I wring out the sponge of energy,
the body that took so much care.

Birds know me, deer raise their heads,
I am walking out into the light.

A NOTE ABOUT THE AUTHOR

David Young is the author of ten previous books of poetry, including *Black Lab* and *At the White Window*. He is a well-known translator of the Chinese poets, and more recently of the poems of Petrarch and Eugenio Montale. A past winner of Guggenheim and NEA fellowships as well as a Pushcart Prize, Young is the Longman Professor Emeritus of English and Creative Writing at Oberlin College and the editor of the Field Poetry Series at Oberlin College Press.

A NOTE ON THE TYPE

This book was set in a typeface named Bulmer. This distinguished letter is a replica of a type long famous in the history of English printing that was designed and cut by William Martin around 1790 for William Bulmer of the Shakespeare Press. In design, it is all but a modern face, with vertical stress, sharp differentiation between the thick and thin strokes, and nearly flat serifs. The decorative italic shows the influence of Baskerville, as Martin was a pupil of John Baskerville's.

Composed by North Market Street Graphics,
Lancaster, Pennsylvania

Printed and bound by Friesens,
Manitoba, Canada

Designed by Soonyoung Kwon